The Time of My Life

DIRTY DANCING MOUNTAIN LAKE MEMOIR

IKE THE BARMAN

Distribution by Bublish, Inc.

ISBN: 978-1-647046-26-2 (eBook)
ISBN: 978-1-647046-27-9 (paperback)

DEDICATION

This book is dedicated to fans the world over of
Dirty Dancing and Mountain Lake. With special
gratitude to Emily, Cliff, Kelley, MD, and G.
Michael, who helped make this book possible.

In memory of Patrick Swayze
August 18, 1952–September 14, 2009

The Patrick Swayze memorial stone at Mountain Lake

ACKNOWLEDGEMENTS

Aside from common knowledge and information culled from visiting geologists, locals, and old hands at the hotel, much of the history recounted in this book was gleaned from Virginia Finnegan Roberts's book *Mountain Lake Remembered* (Favorite Recipes Press, 1994).

A special acknowledgment of gratitude to Valerie Kay Apple, Chef Michael Porterfield, Barbara Fleeman Raines, Carol Lilly, and others who contributed many of the pictures featured in this book. Thanks also to Dave Porter for his excellent work on the maps in chapter 7.

CONTENTS

Welcome to Kellerman's, a.k.a. Mountain Lake Lodge,
Pembroke, Virginia. Photo courtesy of Daniel Stanislowski.

Introduction

My name is Michael Richardson. Some of my friends from across the pond know me as Mike the Barman. Not too long ago I worked at a place called Mountain Lake Lodge, high in the Appalachian Mountains of southwestern Virginia. Many of you reading this book would recognize it better as Kellerman's resort from a little movie called *Dirty Dancing*.

Mike the Barman

For years I was the go-to guy for all things *Dirty Dancing*–related at Mountain Lake, which served as a stand-in for the Catskills of upstate New York. I started working at Mountain Lake in 2001 when my friend, long-time executive chef Mike Porterfield, asked if I could help him out on weekends, as he was desperately understaffed. Though I already had a full-time job as a certified arborist during the week, I readily agreed, and that started an adventure that would transcend fifteen years and generate many memories before I retired to Florida and its warmer winters.

I made it my purpose, as a service to guests, to learn everything there was to know about the movie. Whether it was during an official *Dirty Dancing* weekend at the hotel or just a random day at the resort, I served as the *Dirty Dancing* tour guide, leading both official tours of the property and intimate private tours for überfans. I also ran *Dirty Dancing* trivia contests after screenings of the movie, and other times I was the one who fielded questions asked by guests related to not only the movie but also the history and offerings of the hotel and its surroundings.

It became common practice for the rest of the hotel staff, when asked about either subject, to refer guests to me in the hotel's tavern. The common refrain was "Ask Mike the bartender, he knows everything." Me being me, sometimes I would trick the guests when they asked if I was Mike and tell them I was someone else. Then I would weave an intricate tale of how one day, when Mike could not stand another *Dirty Dancing* question, he quit on the spot and never returned. After gauging the disappointed looks on the guests' faces, I would come clean and admit that I was indeed Mike the Barman. This innocent ruse was made all the easier by the fact that I never wore a name tag while at work. This game was always good for a laugh, for me especially, and the guests didn't seem to mind the subterfuge and enjoyed the levity.

I'll never forget the evening when I was working a routine shift at the hotel and an Englishman entered the tavern. It was a slow weekday, so I was happy for the business. After all, isolated mountain hotels can be underfilled during the off-season, leading to a lot of idle time. What he said to me, however, caused me to pause and take stock.

As was my practice, I naturally greeted the gentleman warmly, asking how he was and if I could help him with anything. He asked if I was Mike the Barman, to which I replied that indeed I was. "Lovely," he replied. "Across the pond, when I told people that I was going to the States, to Virginia, to the place where they filmed *Dirty Dancing*, everyone told me to go and see Mike the Barman—he's the expert on the film." My heart sank. As I meekly smiled at my new friend from the United Kingdom, I thought to myself, *Is this what my life's become?* I was a little taken aback at first. Then I thought, *Hey, my high school guidance counselor said I'd never amount to anything in this lifetime, so I guess he was wrong.*

After that I went all in and sought to give the guests the best *Dirty Dancing* experience I possibly could. That included watching *Dirty Dancing* one thousand seven times over the course of two years, six months, and two weeks. I promise you. I started counting during Christmas of 2015, when I was first asked to screen the movie in the tavern. I wondered how many times the film would be requested by year's end. I just kept on counting after that. Yes, one thousand seven times over the course of two years, six months, and two weeks.

So when I tell you that I am painfully familiar with the movie, you can rest assured that I am. Over the years I sought out every local I could find who was still around and participated in some capacity in the filming of the movie at Mountain Lake. My tailor and dry cleaner in the nearby college town of Blacksburg (home of Virginia Tech) assisted with costumes for the movie. The lady who helped style hair for extras during production came to the tavern a few times while I was working, and I picked her brain for information. The now-grown woman who played the little girl dancing in the gazebo early in the movie also came to the tavern and shared pictures of her with lead choreographer Kenny Ortega and recounted some memories from the time.

I know one of the extras who danced in the gazebo during Penny's dance lesson, and she actually traveled with the crew to film the last dance scene as an extra in Lake Lure, North Carolina. I also count among my friends relatives of the gentleman whose foot Baby steps on in the same gazebo scene, as well as the few remaining staff who were working at the hotel at the time of filming, including Chef Porterfield and his famous motorcycle, which you'll hear more about later. I know the motorcycle well—it sat on the side porch of my former residence near Mountain Lake.

I took meticulous care to closely study the spots at the hotel where filming took place. This is how I know that the placards installed in and around the hotel demarking scene locations fall far short of identifying all the actual places used during the making of the movie over forty-three days during September and October 1986. Research and interviews revealed to me little-known information about very subtle changes the production crew made to the property. For instance, the movie folks planted white pine trees by the kitchen loading dock to obscure it while they were filming. They installed the bollards and chains that line the driveway in front of the hotel to create a look and feel appropriate to the movie's 1963 timeframe. They trucked in sand to create the previously nonexistent beach area by the lake that is so prominent in the background of the wig scene. They also installed the very visible awnings to the front of the stone lodge, which had not previously been there, and had a new gazebo built because they didn't care for the one already there when they arrived to film because it wouldn't have served their needs.

Present day visitors will find the property has been greatly altered since filming occurred. The old horse fencing that lined the road is gone, as is the whitewash that was on all the cabins, changed now to more rustic colors, except for the Virginia Cottage, also affectionately referred to as Baby's Cabin, which now has a different-colored roof. The veranda where Baby casually strolls on her first night at Kellerman's when she first sees Johnny is no longer open to the elements, having been enclosed with mesh screens and french doors. The metal box behind the hotel on the path to the employee housing area where Baby runs into Billy with his arms full of watermelons has since been replaced with a pointed wooden fence, while elsewhere several of the cabins have been removed and replaced with more modern structures. And there is the lake itself, whose water level is much lower than when they filmed the movie. More on that later.

In 2017, which marked the thirtieth anniversary of the release of *Dirty Dancing* in theaters, the hotel swarmed with throngs of movie fans and journalists from all corners of the globe who traveled to southwestern Virginia to celebrate the film. I was interviewed by such diverse publications as *The New York Times*, *Vanity Fair*, and *Baltimore Magazine*, as well as foreign outlets like Germany's *Süddeutsche Zeitung* newspaper and Danish, Dutch, English, and Canadian news and travel publications. I hope when reporters return to document the fortieth anniversary in 2027, the lake will be full.

What I'm trying to do in this book, as best as I can, is to convey the essence of a *Dirty Dancing* weekend via my experiences at Mountain Lake. For those unable to make the pilgrimage to our mountain retreat, I hope this will suffice. For those planning a vacation to the hotel, I hope this memoir serves as a handy reference guide for your future trip. And last, for those who have made the sojourn at some point in past years, I trust it will stir fond memories.

Whatever your situation may be, my intention is to elicit an emotional response in not only those who feel a deep affinity for the movie but also those who love Mountain Lake and this beautiful and inspiring part of the country. I thoroughly enjoyed every moment of my time at the hotel, especially the time I spent interacting with the guests. Admittedly there is a breathtaking beauty to the daybreak on the mountain, and the clear night sky and its blanket of stars are true candy for the soul. But it was the guests I was blessed to meet and befriend that left the most indelible impression on my heart.

Now, together, let's have the time of our lives.

1

A Brief History of Mountain Lake

Any telling of the history of Mountain Lake Lodge and its stories must begin with the lake itself. During its roughly six-thousand-year history, the lake has filled and drained naturally at least seven times. At full pond, the lake is just over fifty-five acres and roughly one hundred feet deep. It's fed constantly by around twenty-four natural freshwater springs that run both under and around the lake, pumping ten thousand–plus gallons of water into the lakebed every day. When we closed for the season in 2008, it had receded to essentially a bathtub's worth of water.

Numerous geologists, hydrologists, biologists, and other scientific types have studied the lake and its surrounding area over the years. The University of Virginia has a biological station near the hotel to monitor lake activity, and I've had the pleasure to converse with many of its researchers over the years. As one of only two naturally occurring lakes in Virginia, and the only natural alpine lake in the southeastern United States, Mountain Lake is among the nation's most fascinating biological destinations.

Mountain Lake in its receded state; the lodge can be seen in the distance from this vantage point near the center of the dry lake

The lake itself formed as the result of what is widely believed to have been a landslide that choked off the outflow from the lake to nearby Doe Creek, which runs roughly parallel to Route 613 down the mountainside. There was still a minimal outflow to Little Stoney Creek, from which

Cascades Falls, a popular hiking destination, receives its water. Core samples taken by multiple researchers from the bottom of the empty lake over the years and the carbon dating of old tree stumps discovered in the dry lake revealed that the lake has drained out completely at least seven times in the past. In fact, the Mountain Lake Lodge tavern is graced by a hemlock stump that was recovered from the lakebed and carved by local artist Bob Evans in 2008.

The lake would have most certainly been familiar to Indigenous peoples before the Columbian exchange, but it wasn't glimpsed by Europeans until 1751, when a gentleman named Christopher Gist chanced upon it at full pond. Yet according to local lore, the second European after Mr. Gist to ascend the mountain and reach the lake reported there was in fact no lake atop the mountain, just a soggy meadow. By 1789 the lake was full again, being surveyed out for the first time.

A series of owners followed, though the property was left largely undeveloped because of the poor nature of the rocky soil, which proved unsuitable for agricultural purposes. In the mid-1850s the first hotel and stagecoach stop were built by the lake at the behest of the landowner, Henley Chapman, following the completion of a turnpike that passed right next to the lake. After the Civil War, Union General Herman Haupt acquired the property, and in 1872 he had an addition put on to the original hotel, doubling its size and capacity. General Haupt sold the hotel and its acreage in 1891. There followed a series of several partnerships that owned the hotel over the years until 1926, when W. L. Moody Jr. of Galveston, Texas, established a partnership with two other gentlemen. By 1930 Mr. Moody had bought out his partners to become the sole owner of the hotel.

Despite the ongoing Great Depression, Mr. Moody decided to build a new hotel completely from scratch to replace the aging structure, parts of which were first milled in 1855. In early 1936, four cottages were demolished and site work began on the new stone hotel. The original hotel continued to receive guests and operate as usual during the season of 1936 while the new building rose nearby. The new lodge went up quickly, and its doors were opened to the public in June 1937. The old hotel was dismantled, and its wood was used to build the barn and several cottages— some still stand, but others have been removed and replaced with newer structures. Stonemasons, many of whom were refugees fleeing the carnage of the Spanish Civil War, then constructed the stone building, which also features some wood from the old hotel. The stone building now houses the hotel gift shop and outfitters; the new clubhouse up on the old golf course, which opened in 1917 and closed in the mid-1980s; and the aforementioned biological station.

Mr. Moody, at one point one of the richest men in America, remained the sole owner of the property until he passed away in 1954. Along with Mountain Lake, Mr. Moody's portfolio included Affiliated National Hotel Company, with twenty-four hotels nationwide; American National Insurance Company; and forty-eight other companies. His daughter, Mary Moody Northen—whose husband, Edwin Clyde Northen, also passed away in 1954—inherited all her father's interests.

Mary loved Mountain Lake. From childhood she spent her summers at the lake almost every year, until her death in Galveston in 1986. Mary had no children of her own, so to ensure Mountain Lake would be enjoyed by future generations, she deeded the hotel and its property to a philanthropic organization she founded in 1964 called the Mary Moody Northen Endowment, which still retains title to the hotel and its 2,600-acre nature preserve.

Then one day, shortly after Mary's death, on a seemingly normal day in September 1986, a movie crew showed up to shoot a flick that nobody had much hope for. Known actors had been offered plum roles but had turned them down. Musicians reluctantly recorded songs they were convinced would be bombs. Staff at the hotel muttered to themselves that if the old lady had still been alive, she would never have allowed it to happen. Especially a low-budget film that was being produced by Vestron, a company best known for straight-to-video fare. They filmed a movie that seemed destined for the same fate.

But it would prove otherwise—and the rest is history.

2

Buzz and the Chef

WE OWE IT ALL TO BUZZ

Dirty Dancing weekends at Mountain Lake—and the many stories I'll be sharing with you—were made possible by a wonderful gentleman affectionately known as Buzz. Horace "Buzz" Scanland Jr. was the much-beloved general manager at Mountain Lake Hotel for many years. His tenure at the hotel began on the day filming of *Dirty Dancing* commenced in September 1986.

Buzz began his service to the hotel in the sales office, before transitioning to the position of general manager in 1988. Until his retirement at the conclusion of the season in 2012, he was ever present on the mountain, assuring and steady in his duties. And when I say ever present, I mean ever present. Before 2013 the hotel operated on a seasonal basis, open from Mother's Day weekend until the Sunday following Thanksgiving. Even when the hotel was closed to guests during the winter months, Buzz could be found on site Monday through Friday, and few snowstorms could dissuade him from coming to work.

Longtime Mountain Lake general manager Buzz Scanland works the crowd during the event he created, *Dirty Dancing* Themed Weekends

Before Buzz became general manager there was no official *Dirty Dancing* experience of any kind. He essentially created the *Dirty Dancing* weekend from scratch, not so much out of any great demand but to enhance guests' overall experience at Mountain Lake. To be certain, *Dirty Dancing* fans made the pilgrimage to the hotel before themed weekends were a thing, but they wandered aimlessly around the property, searching on their own for filming sites. Before Buzz, many of the guests missed key movie locations or misidentified others. Sometimes they thought scenes filmed at

Lake Lure in North Carolina (more on that later) were shot at Mountain Lake or vice versa. Buzz recognized a need and as was his way, addressed it to the benefit and enjoyment of guests and visiting fans.

Buzz arranged—with the consent of Lionsgate, the company that owns the film rights to *Dirty Dancing*—to create an experience at the hotel that guests were sure to enjoy and not soon forget. Through his diligence, *Dirty Dancing*–themed memorabilia and trinkets soon filled the hotel gift shop's shelves and racks. In short time visitors were proudly sporting *Dirty Dancing*–emblazoned shirts, sweatpants, hoodies, and hats. Anything that was appropriate was sold featuring the *Dirty Dancing* logo or quotes from the movie. Buzz oversaw the installation of markers to denote the exact location of filming areas so guests could easily locate sites on their own. And even though the iconic bridge scene was filmed at Lake Lure, to enhance the guest experience, Buzz had a bridge built above the hotel, on the path to Bald Knob, so fans could stage their own reenactments for photo opportunities. Most importantly, Buzz initiated the official *Dirty Dancing* tour. Guests who attended *Dirty Dancing* weekends back in the days when Buzz ran the hotel always remember him very fondly. I would be so bold as to posit that Buzz was the father of the *Dirty Dancing* experience at Mountain Lake.

The tour that Buzz developed served as the template for the one I performed, which the guests always assured me was one of the highlights of their *Dirty Dancing* weekends, so I have to say, I owe it all to him. Like the kindly grandfather figure that he was, he would personally lead the tour on the official weekend, enthralling the guests with his insightful knowledge of movie sites and anecdotes from when the production crew was here. The guests loved it beyond description.

Back in those days Buzz led the tours through the kitchen so the fans could see Penny's spot—the place where Baby sees Penny weeping as an unaware Neil offers up beets or cabbage rolls from a refrigerator—and the cooking line used during the filming of the kitchen scenes. Every guest could have their picture taken where Penny was crying, and many fans tried their best to work up tears in homage to the moment. One of Buzz's tours caught me cutting watermelon in the kitchen, creating a scene that helped shape what became the "Secret Tour"—more on that in chapter 5.

Obligatory watermelons on the front lawn of the
hotel during a *Dirty Dancing* weekend

Buzz was also the driving force behind the excavation, engraving, and installation of the Patrick Swayze memorial stone, which was extracted from the lake near where the water lift scene was filmed. A photo of the stone can be seen on the dedication page at the front of this book.

Buzz was always devoted to the guest experience. His desk was just inside the door of the executive offices on the ground floor of the hotel. Buzz forswore a private office so he could always be available. On weekends he could be found either interacting with diners in the dining room, especially during the brunch on Sundays, or hobnobbing with guests one-on-one in the library (now the tavern) or in the lobby. He knew and remembered names and faces and was always quick with a greeting, a handshake, or a pat on the shoulder. Buzz had a warm way of making everyone feel like family. Aside from the *Dirty Dancing* experience he created, he also was integral to the fruition of another true guest favorite: Oktoberfest.

Oktoberfest was something to behold. For almost two decades, upward of two hundred fifty to three hundred revelers a night would crowd into the barn for old-world food, beer, fun, and music. Buzz found a German-style oompah band, which on some nights numbered almost twenty-four members, each dressed in traditional Bavarian-style lederhosen and felt hats or traditional German maiden dresses, who played traditional German folk music into the night after the feast. Much German beer was consumed on those nights. Oktoberfest started each year on the second-to-last weekend in September and continued every weekend in October for a total of twelve nights a year. There was always a whole smoked pig, sauerbraten, potato pancakes, schnitzel, and so much sausage with so much more. It was big.

One year, though it may sound unlikely, executives from a brewery in Bavaria traveled to the hotel. It seems that for six weeks every year (our Oktoberfest), Mountain Lake sold more of their beer than any other place on the US Eastern Seaboard. This anomaly had apparently been going on for years, and although impressed, the executives couldn't understand why a place that didn't appear on their maps sold so much of their beer. They decided to investigate in person, and during their stay at Mountain Lake they must have liked what they saw, because one night they picked up everybody's bar tab, totaling around twenty-five thousand dollars.

Sadly Buzz is no longer with us, having passed away in December 2018. He will always be missed by those who knew him or served under him at the hotel. He left an indelible, positive mark there, one that will be hard for anyone to surpass. To me and many who worked with him, he will always be remembered as "that very nice man."

MY FRIEND THE CHEF

The Chef, G. Michael Porterfield, is an institution unto himself at Mountain Lake. Over the course of three separate stints, spread over nearly four decades, he has come to symbolize a comforting sense of continuity, while his culinary fare presents all that is tasty and delicious at the old stone hotel. To add to his bona fides, he's one of the very few staff still working at the hotel who were also present when the movie was filmed. The Chef started working at Mountain Lake in the early 1980s as garde-manger, before working his way up to the position of sous chef. He personally prepared meals for Mary Moody Northen before her passing in 1986, the year *Dirty Dancing* was filmed.

Chef Porterfield left the hotel in 1992, under very good terms, to take the position of chef de cuisine at Roanoke College in nearby Salem, Virginia. In 2001 Buzz asked Chef Porterfield to return to Mountain Lake to be the new executive chef. The Chef supervised not only preparation for the food to be served in the dining room but also the numerous cookouts, Oktoberfest fare, countless conclaves and banquets, and up to three weddings a day on the weekends. It was crazy busy back then, but he had good help, and everything generally ran very smoothly. Sadly, after the lake took its dirt nap in 2008 business fell off dramatically. In 2012, at the close of the season, the Chef again left the hotel, following Buzz's retirement. By 2015, following the less-than-stellar performance of a succession of three different executive chefs, Chef Porterfield was asked to return yet again to Mountain Lake. He has helmed the kitchen ever since, delighting guests with his ample and creative culinary fare.

As I mentioned, the Chef was working at the hotel during the filming of *Dirty Dancing*, so I plumbed his deep well of knowledge and memories of that time to assist mightily in the preparation for this book. Readily and affably, he regaled me with countless stories, which are peppered throughout. Chef Porterfield's roots run truly deep at Mountain Lake. At the turn of the twentieth century his ancestors owned Mountain Lake Hotel with partners. The hotel has in essence always been home to him. It's in his blood. And with his food, he has always tried to impart Mountain Lake's essence to each and every guest.

For *Dirty Dancing* weekends the Chef would always put out hearty spreads for the fans. The cornucopia of food he prepared was truly mind-boggling. The breakfast buffets featured fresh pancakes, french toast, fried potatoes, juicy link sausage, sausage gravy, biscuits, bacon ranging from medium rare to brittle, eggs, fruit, bagels . . . I could go on, but you get the picture. Of course, if a guest requested an omelet or something else, the Chef would happily oblige, and all the meals were included in the *Dirty Dancing* weekend package.

Lunch buffets featured a vast array of choices, including green and chilled salads, hot meats, pastas, vegetables, the works. I used to assure the guests that if they couldn't find something they enjoyed, I would personally go outside and collect nuts and berries for them to eat if that was more to their liking. There were never any takers. But the consistent feature of every *Dirty Dancing* weekend was always the giant sandwich. This monster was a goliath of meat, cheese, lettuce, tomato, onions, peppers, and so much more. The sandwich measured five feet in length and a little over a foot tall. The Chef would ensure that there were no less than three of these sandwiches for each *Dirty Dancing* weekend lunch and would stand out in the dining room and hand carve slices of this super dagwood, much to the delight of the enthusiastic guests. During my stay in the kitchen, I made one once, and I assure you it was no easy task to make one of these, much less three. Picture slicing mounds of turkey, ham, salami, capicola, roast beef, corned beef, swiss, cheddar, provolone, tomatoes, onions, and lettuce . . . whew.

The Chef on an official *Dirty Dancing* weekend behind what's left of one of the giant sandwiches he made for lunch

Dinner was, again, a smorgasbord. I cannot begin to give the due to the Chef that he deserves with his varied hot and succulent offerings, which included cold salads, breads, and desserts. Every dinner service the Chef would be front and center once again, carving to order, only now it would be juicy prime rib or steamship round and beef tenderloin, depending on the night. Always he smiled and served the guests as much sliced beef as they could want or carry. If there ever came a complaint about the food he served on *Dirty Dancing* weekends, it never reached my or anyone else's ears. After all, how can you complain about being offered everything wonderful? And yes, there was always pot roast, very tender and juicy I might add. It was, after all, the only food other than watermelon mentioned in the movie.

During the old days when Buzz would lead the tours through the kitchen and then out the back door onto the loading dock, the Chef would follow the last guest outside and recount his memories of the making of the movie at the hotel to the assembled crowd. I was never able to go out and watch his presentation since those of us in the kitchen had to scramble to get the lunch buffet ready to go out, but judging from the cheers and applause, his stories were well received by the guests. One thing I know, however, is that the Chef would always assure fans that Patrick Swayze was a really nice guy. The Chef would talk to people about drinking beer with Mr. Swayze and several of the other hotel staff at the time, as well as patrons and film crew members. Mr. Swayze also seemed to bum cigarettes quite a bit, but then, he was a blue-collar guy and not only approachable but also very friendly.

Another tale the Chef would tell, much to the delight of guests and movie fans, is the famous motorcycle story. I know the motorcycle well—a 1983 Suzuki GR650, it sat on the porch of the house where I lived, near the resort. According to the Chef, Mr. Swayze missed the last shuttle to Blacksburg after filming had wrapped up one day and needed a ride to his hotel in Blacksburg. Remember, this was a low-budget movie with a relatively unknown cast, Jerry Orbach being the most famous of the actors in the movie at the time, and there was fairly short notice to Mountain Lake staff that a large movie entourage was coming (more on that later). Throughout the production, we still had incoming guests with long-standing reservations to attend to, which limited the availability of rooms at the hotel, so many of the actors and crew had to stay in Blacksburg from time to time, Mr. Swayze among them. And on this day, he needed a ride.

Chef Porterfield and his famous motorcycle

Enter the Chef, who gladly offered to give Mr. Swayze a lift to town on his motorcycle. According to the Chef, Mr. Swayze didn't mind riding on a motorcycle, but he wanted to drive. The Chef demurred, so Mr. Swayze found himself on the back of the Chef's Suzuki, heading down Route 700, which winds for seven miles, has almost no guardrails, is not particularly wide, and features 2,200 feet of elevation change. The Chef knew the road very well, and despite the forty-five-mile-per-hour speed limit, regularly raced up and down at speeds closer to sixty miles per hour.

Mr. Swayze started the trip to Blacksburg holding on to the bar on the back of the seat, assuring Chef he wasn't afraid of going fast. By the third curve he had both of his arms wrapped securely around the Chef's midriff. They rode like that all seven miles to the bottom—and the final ten miles to Blacksburg thereafter. Once they got to the hotel, Mr. Swayze jokingly told the Chef that he could tell all his friends that he gave Patrick Swayze a ride on his motorcycle, to which the Chef replied that Mr. Swayze could tell all his friends that he got a ride from Mike Porterfield.

Patrick Swayze on site at Mountain Lake in 1986

Aside from the immoveable structures, and the mountain itself, the Chef is the closest thing there is to continuity at the hotel. Even the lake leaves from time to time. He is the thread that connects time through the decades. Always pleasant with the guests and willing to engage fans with his insight into *Dirty Dancing* and the hotel, he's kind of a living monument. If you should ever find yourself able to make the trek up the mountain to the hotel, I encourage you to seek him out, say hello, and ask him to tell you some stories about Mountain Lake of yore.

3

What to Expect When You're Expecting Guests

W hat to expect when you're expecting guests: anything and everything, especially on a *Dirty Dancing* weekend. To say the movie has some of the most devoted and fervent fans in the world would be a gross understatement. Before I became the bartender, when I worked for the Chef doing banquets and making omelets, I thought I had an inkling of the fan base and their love of the movie. But when I shifted out to the tavern, I realized I didn't know anything. This chapter is in no way meant to impugn any of the movie fans or guests; they were and are the lifeblood of the hotel, and God bless each and every one of them. But before I get into details of the *Dirty Dancing* tour in later chapters, I thought it would be fun to recount some of the more extreme and humorous examples of human behavior I encountered during my tenure at the hotel. I truly hope no one takes any offense because none is intended.

The more die-hard movie fans would steal anything even remotely *Dirty Dancing* related, actual or perceived. From the old markers that denoted where the movie scenes had been filmed to just about anything portable out of room 232, where Patrick Swayze stayed during filming (see chapter 4). But it didn't end there. Occasionally I would arrive at work in the tavern only to find that some light-fingered fan had slipped behind the bar in the dead of night during the few hours that I had gone home and helped themselves to either a few pages of a copy of the script or the whole thing. That's why I always kept extra copies of the script in my car. They vanished not just on the *Dirty Dancing* weekends but on other random days as well. I had to be prepared—I was in the hospitality business after all. That's light lifting. Other fans would trek onto the lakebed and take cinder blocks, which were not even vaguely associated with the movie. Now that's tenacity. Some folks tried to pry up parts of the dance floor in Mary's Barn, even though it wasn't installed until 2007. And people were caught from time to time trying to chip away bits of the stone hotel for whatever reason.

Most fans were more deferential than those guests. They were just happy to walk around the grounds where the movie that means so much to them was filmed and, in a small way, perhaps, feel like they were part of it. Then there are fans I refer to as "Those". By "Those" I mean the super-über-mega fans, who sometimes behaved like it was their first time out of the house. It didn't take long working at the bar for me to get a firsthand taste of how emotional and intense a very small segment of the fan base can become. But then, that's true of almost anything, be it politics, religion, nature, or even cupcakes. I'll take up "Those" in a bit, but first I'd like to talk about the vast majority of guests who came because of the movie.

On *Dirty Dancing* weekends the guests could be divided into several distinct groups. Now I'm not saying this to stereotype anyone, and there's certainly nothing scientific about my observations. They're just that: observations. But to be honest with you, time taught me that my observations were generally spot-on. Very seldom did female guests attend the *Dirty Dancing* festivities by themselves. They might arrive solo, but they were soon joined by expected friends. Mostly they would arrive in pairs or in threesomes. These weekends were their getaways, girls' weekends, escapes from their husbands and children. For a few days they could meet old friends and relive their younger days, if for nothing less, to preserve their sanity. Many planned their trips no less than a year ahead and waited with anticipation for the weekend to finally arrive.

Couples were the next most prevalent attendees and guests. Married, engaged, or just dating, they came for the romantic aspect of the hotel and the mood the *Dirty Dancing* weekends would create. Most often the trip to the hotel came as a total surprise for the ladies. It was nice to see so frequently that romance was alive and well. Trickery of a sort was often involved. The gentleman would, knowing his paramour's love for the movie, secretly book a weekend at the hotel without her knowledge. What excuses they would concoct to drive into the middle of nowhere I cannot imagine, but the subterfuge seemed to work well. As they would get closer to the hotel, many of the men would surreptitiously start to play the soundtrack to the movie, hinting slyly that something was going to happen. Seldom did the women pick up the subtleties, as they would breathlessly confess to me, expressing their shock and delight when they realized where they were. Of course, upon arrival most of the ladies quickly grasped where they were and became very excited. For others it took a few minutes for where they were to sink in. Regardless, I cannot recall anyone being disappointed by the surprise destination. A few babies were probably conceived at Mountain Lake during my tenure at the bar, but I cannot say for certain.

The mother-daughter couples were a different pairing altogether. Of all the varied configurations, the mothers and daughters were the most likely to while away the hours sitting in the tavern, watching the movie replay hour after hour, seemingly disinterested in anything else. Admittedly, they would often sally outside after several viewings on non–*Dirty Dancing* weekends to take pictures of the sites. But on the official weekends, after the tour, they would often just stay in the tavern watching the movie play hour after hour. As always, I would apprise them of the sites not listed on the scene map provided at the front desk, including those off property, and they would be thankful. Sometimes they would venture off the mountain, down to the Cascades waterfall, searching for a log they could photograph and pass off as the one from the movie. But after that it was back to the tavern to watch the movie again and again.

The larger groups, which consisted of anywhere between four and twenty women, came across to me as guests on a mission, so to speak. They never missed any of the preplanned activities on the *Dirty Dancing* weekends. Be it the tour, the lawn games, the bingo, the movie and subsequent trivia, the dance lessons, or the big dance, they were always in a group. They ate together at every meal and were generally inseparable the whole weekend. This was readily apparent because they always wore the same matching outfits. Almost always they had brought their own, either purchased online, procured somewhere close to home, or crafted by one or all of them. Many of the outfits were very personalized, sparkly, and definitely flamboyant, with some bearing their own *Dirty Dancing* nicknames. Sometimes they bore numbers on their backs, like a sports jersey. The color schemes encompassed everything imaginable, though black and pink were the predominant themes.

I found that the larger the group, the more likely it was that they had traveled together, either by caravan or flight, while groups of between four and eight generally traveled from different locations, usually arriving separately but becoming inseparable once they reunited at the hotel. There were exceptions to the travel arrangements, but that was my takeaway from interacting with so many guests. Several times the larger groups enjoying the *Dirty Dancing* weekends also doubled as special occasions, be they birthdays, sorority reunions, or bachelorette parties. The latter could get a little boisterous from time to time, though many guests also did on *Dirty Dancing* weekends. That was accepted, so long as it didn't get too out of hand. Mountain Lake, located as it is high atop a mountain in the middle of a rural county in southwestern Virginia, is not a place most people are inclined to leave after dark if they've been drinking. Besides, after nine at night most of the sidewalks in Giles County have been rolled up and put away for the night so they don't get wet.

Last are the single men. Many are true, dyed-in-the-wool fans who are just as nostalgic as any of the women. Some, however, I couldn't help but wonder about. The single guys would come into the bar, loiter, maybe have a drink, and scan the crowd to see what there was to see before meandering off. Often they would pass through the tavern multiple times over the course of the day to see if the faces had changed. The single men were always at the dances—that's where the ladies were. I often wondered if these gentlemen booked the *Dirty Dancing* weekends in anticipation of a target-rich environment. Sorry, fellas, almost all of them are already married.

Changing course briefly, I was always amused by the number of guests who were shaken up by the drive to the hotel on Routes 700 and 613, and there were a lot. Heck, I passed more cars on Route 700 than I can count, even though it has double solid lines for its entire length. Despite the speed limit being forty-five miles per hour, people would putter up and down the hill at twenty to twenty-five miles per hour. I never had time for that slow of a speed, and I didn't want to burn up my brakes by riding behind a flat-lander creeping up or down the mountain. Guests found it hard to believe the road was drivable at sixty miles per hour in most places below the overlook. I often offered to bring my car around and show them how quickly it could be driven if they wanted to ride along, but nobody accepted my offer.

The constant complaint I heard about the ride up Route 700 was the lack of guardrails, and indeed there are only three short segments the entire seven miles. I would assure them that despite the dearth of guardrails, the trees that lined the road would stop them eventually. Many guests, upon arrival at the hotel, were literally quite jittery from the drive up. I had so many guests come straight into the bar, forgoing check-in for the time being, to have a drink to steady their nerves from all the twists and turns and from the altitude change. Ears would pop on their way up, a sensation some had never experienced before visiting the hotel. Sometimes I would recommend to the guests a nice day trip off the mountain to visit the nearby Cascades, or maybe lunch or a canoe rental down in Pembroke. I would talk about Blacksburg, a charming town, or the Appalachian Trail and other pleasant places to visit to mix things up. I was told by well more than a few guests that they were definitely not getting into their car and driving off the mountain until they checked out. Once up and down the mountain was a lifetime's worth for them.

Urbanites from the northern areas, especially the Philadelphia, New York, and Boston metro areas, are the funniest guests though. One of my favorite recollections involves three visitors from New York City. They came directly into the tavern, ordered drinks, and promptly asked what was up with the road. I told them that there was nothing wrong with the road, it worked just fine. Then one of the guests asked where the guardrails were. I replied, as usual, that there were three segments and that where there were none, the trees would stop them from going too far off the road. Another of the group then asked where the streetlights were. I must admit I was a little taken aback. I tried to explain just how rural the area was, but it just didn't seem to sink in. No matter how politely I tried to explain the logistical impossibility of having streetlights in such a remote area, they just couldn't quite fathom the ridiculousness of their question. They were adamant that winding roads should have illumination, just like the straight streets of New York did. What a fun and amusing group they were. Another amusing trait that city people exhibited was their amazement at how friendly folks in the South are. They were constantly bewildered that once they crossed the Mason–Dixon line, perfect strangers would greet them or hold the door for them for no other reason than to be polite. City folk are funny, I must confess.

I did have a word of caution for guests, sometimes unfortunately delivered too late, but always greatly appreciated: don't speed in Virginia in general and Giles County in particular. I've driven all over this country, sometimes crossing whole states without seeing one constable. Not in Virginia. Almost from the moment you cross the state line, police can be seen patrolling the highways or hiding in little cutouts, and quite frequently at that. Giles is worse, by far. I recommend that guests set the cruise control five miles per hour over the posted speed limit and enjoy the beautiful scenery of Virginia and Giles County. And for the love of all that is good and wholesome, do not speed through the little town of Pembroke in Giles County. If you're traveling from the west on Route 460 approaching Pembroke, the speed limit falls from sixty to forty-five miles per hour. They are not kidding. Ninety percent of guests who received traffic citations received them in Pembroke, a town of a little over one thousand souls, but with five sworn officers. There's only one way to pay for all those officers, and that's by pulling over speeders.

The nature and enthusiasm of how each guest reacted to being at the home of *Dirty Dancing* ran the whole gamut. Once, early in my tenure at the tavern, I was at the bar, and it being summer, I had the french doors on the veranda open for the cool breeze. I heard a woman scream, so naturally I ran outside, where the shriek had come from. The lady was on the sidewalk beside her car, on her knees. I ran down to her and checked to see if she was okay. Tears were streaming down her cheeks, lots and lots of tears. I thought that maybe she was having a stroke or heart attack or worse, but when I asked, she blubbered how happy she was to be at the hotel, her voice broken and choked. It was her lifelong dream, she said, to come and see where the movie had been filmed. That's when I realized that she was one of "Those". Nothing wrong with that. A little intense for me, but hey, I was in the hospitality business, so if the guests were happy, I was happy.

That guest was one of my most vivid recollections of an überfan, but there were so many others who passed through the hotel's doors. Some would come in and touch everything, and I do mean everything, asking if Patrick Swayze had touched the same surface, or this or that surface. They

27

would sit on every piece of furniture, asking if he might have once graced it with his backside, or which of the bar stools was his favorite. I would break the news that the tavern was at the time of filming a library and that we didn't have a bar when they were making the movie. If possible, I would take them up to room 232 to placate them if it was unoccupied.

The more persistent were the guests who would plant themselves at the bar and sit there for hours picking my brain to pieces about any tidbit of movie or Patrick Swayze trivia or gossip. Since the movie played on what seemed like an endless loop while I was working, I would point out the bloopers and editing gaffes to everyone (see chapter 10), but for some reason, the more die-hard fans seemed to believe that I had some sort of special insight into the film because I seemed to know so much about it. Truth be told, some trivia about the movie I picked up by myself, some was pointed out to me by guests or staff, while the rest, including the history of the hotel, I read. They sell a little Mountain Lake history book at the front desk and gift shop, which I read numerous times on slow nights at work. I gave the persistent "Those" everything I had, but it was never enough. Many times some of the guests felt I was holding back information, but I never was. It got a little frustrating, but again, I was in the hospitality business.

4

Room 232

n the hotel proper, up the staircase on the second floor, is room 232, which has come to be called Patrick Swayze's room. The room is at a T intersection of hallways, but from the top of the stairs, looking left, appears to be at the end of the hall. To be sure, Patrick Swayze did indeed stay in that room for a few days, but what most folks are unaware of is that the movie crew didn't take over the whole hotel while they were here. Production of the movie at Mountain Lake was last minute, so to speak, and as such there were numerous other guests who had reserved rooms well in advance of the production crew's arrival whose reservations had to be honored. Also, there were more of the movie people than the small hotel could accommodate anyway, so off-site hotels had to be used as a recourse. Hotel rooms were secured in Blacksburg and elsewhere for the movie crew.

The only reason we know for certain that Patrick Swayze stayed in room 232 is because somehow, across all these years,

two pages from the sign-in ledger survived from September
1 and 2, 1986. I always provided guests with photocop-
ies of the ledger sheet featuring Patrick Swayze's signature.
Along with Patrick Swayze's signature, the names of Cynthia
Rhodes (Penny); Miranda Garrison (Vivian); Jennifer Grey
(Baby), though she signed in as Jennifer Gilbert; Kenny
Ortega, the principal choreographer; and screenwriter
Eleanor Bergstein also appear. Jerry Orbach, who played
Dr. Houseman, didn't check in until September 3, which is
noted at the bottom of the ledger page dated September 2.

A copy of the hotel's ledger page from September 1986, with
Patrick Swayze's signature and the signatures of other cast and
crew members from when they checked into the hotel

Several years ago some lovely ladies visiting the United States from Iceland came to the hotel (by the way, people from Iceland prefer to be called Icelandic, not Icelanders, as I was assured when they corrected me). Having given each of the guests a copy of the sign-in ledger, they asked about a particular name on the list, which previously I had never noticed, or at least paid no attention to. The name was Frida Aradottir, and they insisted that it sounded very Icelandic. I didn't even need to feign ignorance because I had no idea. Quickly they turned to the information cure-all, Google, and in seconds determined the name was indeed Icelandic in origin. It turns out she was the principal hairdresser for *Dirty Dancing*. Later she would go on to work on such films as *Jurassic Park* and *La La Land*, along with a host of other movies over the years. Small world, small movie, huge impact.

But back to room 232. It is almost impossible to recount all the stories I accrued from taking guests up to see the room. I'm still amazed at how a simple, no-frills room in an old stone hotel attracts such reverence. Innumerable times did I lead guests up there and open the room for viewing only to find yet again that the visitors became flush with excitement. Their level of fascination never ceased to amaze me. As with the memorial rock out by the gazebo, if I had a dollar for every time mature women behaved like fawning teenagers, I would be doing very well. For instance, I cannot count the number of times I was handed guests' cell phones and asked, and I quote, "Take my picture. I'm on Patrick Swayze's throne," as they perched themselves on the toilet in 232's bathroom.

The hallway leading to room 232 where Patrick Swayze stayed briefly, as seen from the top of the stairs on the second floor

The door to room 232 at Mountain Lake Hotel

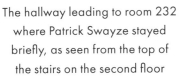

Other times they would hand me their cell phones and hop into the bathtub and pretend to be showering or even bathing. Most often the ladies would sprawl on the bed and pose provocatively as if they were awaiting the imminent embrace of Johnny Castle and the impending loss of their innocence. That happened a lot. Thankfully, most guests just took pictures of the room, marveling at how simple and unpretentious it was. I think it gave solace to many of the guests knowing that Patrick Swayze was a blue-collar guy who didn't need the trappings of celebrity to be comfortable.

The biggest issue with room 232, however, was the bi-
zarre desire of some guests to remove items from the room.
Over the years the shower curtain in room 232 disappeared
from the bathroom innumerable times. Come on, really,
people? First, a thirty-year-old shower curtain would just be
disgusting, I don't care how often it was cleaned. Second,
who in their right mind would want an old (or even new)
shower curtain? It doesn't make any sense whatsoever. But
as I related to guests over the years, the fanatics will take
anything even vaguely related, no matter how improbable,
to the movie. Along with the perpetually vanishing shower
curtains, though rarely, the toilet seat itself was known to
disappear. As did the bedding, towels, and other sundries
over the years. I realize it sounds odd, but literally, there are
people, wherever they may be from, who have an overriding
compulsion to possess something, anything, that they feel
Patrick Swayze might have come in contact with, if even just
momentarily.

A few years ago somebody actually took the time to remove the decorative room number plate from the hallway
door of room 232. This plate had been secured to the door
since the 1930s. One day it was there, the next it was gone.
This took some effort, as the screws affixing the small brass
plate to the door were quite long and deeply embedded.
The front desk staff printed up a small strip of paper with
the number 232 on it so guests could find the room and
secured it to the door using Scotch tape. In less than half a
year that little strip of paper had to be replaced at least six
times. It is, after all, easier to remove paper and Scotch tape
than a deeply secured brass plate.

But even that doesn't take the cake. I brought some ladies up one evening to show them the room, and as we proceeded down the corridor, I kept thinking that there was something odd about the door, missing brass number plate notwithstanding. I couldn't quite figure what was off about the door until we got to it. That's when I realized that somebody had stolen the peephole. The peephole! Who does that? What could you possibly do with a peephole? Did they need one for their home? I assume the prospect of Patrick Swayze's eyelashes brushing against it in the past compelled someone to take it.

Even without the original number placard, I still took numerous pictures of guests standing in front of the door, pointing at the strip of paper reading "232." Ironically, the room still displays a No Smoking sign on the door, one of the few that still do at the hotel. It's ironic because Patrick Swayze smoked cigarettes until he passed away, though when they were filming *Dirty Dancing*, smoking was allowed everywhere in the hotel.

5

The Secret Tour

BEFORE IT WAS SECRET

B ack in the old days, up until 2013, the official *Dirty Dancing* tour included a segment that would later become what I called the secret tour. Guests would come through the kitchen and be afforded the opportunity to have their picture taken in what we called Penny's spot—the place where Penny sits weeping while Neil offers Baby food from a refrigerator. Baby deftly steers Neil away, forgoing the brownies or sweet gherkins, and then runs to the gazebo to fetch Billy and Johnny. Since the tour came into the kitchen between breakfast service and lunch, we would do a quick clean, especially in Penny's spot, before the guests would come in. Since it was a working kitchen, some of the staff would be scrubbing furiously, while others would be prepping for the next meal. The Chef would mount a light (actually a clampable heat lamp) so there would be proper illumination, and then, one by one, guests would file through to have their picture taken, doing their best weeping Penny impression, before proceeding on through to the back loading dock for the next segment of the tour.

When the last guest had left the kitchen, that was the cue for the Chef to join Buzz, the general manager who led the tours back then, on the back dock. The Chef would use this segment of the tour to regale the guests with his tales of the time when they filmed the movie. The guests always enjoyed hearing his firsthand memories of interactions with the movie people and recollections of what it was like when they shot the film back in 1986. The Chef is a colorful character in his own right and adept at telling a tale and spinning a yarn.

Back then I used to work only weekends and help out at banquets, special events like the *Dirty Dancing* weekends and weddings, the Oktoberfests, and any other festivities and functions. I was also the omelet maker for our busy Sunday brunches. It was the Chef's cruel joke on me, as he knew I hated eggs, but I was in the hospitality business, so I gave it my all. One Sunday the assistant chef who used to carve the prime rib and baked ham on the buffet, Big Jack, challenged me to offer twenty-five possible ingredients for omelets. I managed over seventy. If you wanted a hot dog omelet that day, I had you covered.

The tours always happened on Saturday, between break-fast and lunch, as I've mentioned, which led to a very interesting development one day. Buzz was leading the tour, as always, and came into the kitchen with the group, each member eagerly awaiting their turn to get their picture in

Penny's nook. My workstation was just opposite the nook. I was busily cutting up fresh fruit for the lunch buffet, and just as I was about to start slicing up a whole, fresh watermelon, one of the guests asked if she could have her picture taken with the melon. Bear in mind, this was well before I was as thoroughly acquainted with the movie as I am now, and so, a little sarcastically, I asked if she was aware that this melon was not from 1986. She looked at me like I was a moron.

Needless to say, everybody ended up manhandling that watermelon that day. Folks who had already taken pictures of the nook and passed through to the loading dock returned to take pictures of themselves holding the watermelon. The tour that day was almost forty-five minutes longer than usual, as everyone had to be photographed cradling the melon in their arms. It kind of threw a wrench in the works and delayed the whole weekend schedule. After that we made sure to have multiple fresh watermelons readily available in the kitchen for opportunistic photographs and were able to get the tour back on track.

Later someone had the brilliant idea to just get a pallet of sugar baby melons and place them out on the front lawn for guests, thereby sparing the kitchen of the imposition and allowing us to get on with our primary task of feeding the guests. The pallet idea worked well for a while. Indeed, during *Dirty Dancing* weekends it spawned a new lawn game: the watermelon toss. It was quite popular, and the guests loved standing before the stone hotel building holding and tossing melons and being photographed. Unfortunately the law of unintended consequences came into play.

With a watermelon toss, as with any produce-related recreational activity, sometimes the fruit hits the ground. Many a melon made contact not with human hands but with the ground, where they would burst open. It was quite amusing when it initially occurred, but then there came the unintended consequences that I alluded to. Broken fresh fruit tends to attract insects, namely flying, yellow-and-black, striped stinging insects. It got a little ugly one weekend. Many guests, who were at first giggling at the sight of all that smashed produce, found themselves swarmed by wasps and yellow jackets attracted to the sugary flesh of the broken melons. Guests panicked, running about swatting at the gathering insects and seeking shelter. Several guests were stung, though not so seriously that anyone required medical treatment. That was the last time we set out pallets of sugar baby melons or encouraged watermelons to be tossed as a lawn game.

Despite the drawbacks of encouraging glad-handing of fresh produce on the hotel grounds, the innocuous melon is still associated with Mountain Lake. Countless guests, and even casual day visitors, would stop off at a nearby store and purchase a watermelon just to have a prop for photographs when they drove up to the hotel. They would carry them all over the property, snapping pictures at every available place they could recognize from the movie. Then they would abandon the melon, leaving it on the back loading dock of the kitchen. I cannot even begin to pretend to know how many times I walked out the back of the hotel kitchen to find, once again, that the watermelon fairy had made yet another visit. During the busy summer months, many a slice of watermelon was served at the hotel, though seldom did we have to buy a watermelon.

BIRTH OF THE SECRET TOUR

In 2013 there was a change of management at the hotel, and Buzz reluctantly went into retirement. After his departure the tours were usually directed by some ill-informed member of the recreation staff, who read from a poorly prepared script. By the time I took up the mantle the tour was in shambles. All Buzz had done for so long had gone to rot. I did what I could, but the new food and beverage director had gotten it into his mind that the kitchen part of the tour was, for extremely vague reasons and rationale, no longer part of the program. It made no sense to many of us old hands. But for better or worse, for the time being, he was the boss. For many guests it was for the worse.

One day the director's head exploded (in restaurant parlance), and he departed abruptly. Before his departure I had already started the secret tour however, and I kept it up until the day I left myself. But first I must tell you how it all began.

As I've mentioned, I had spent several years at the hotel in whatever capacity the Chef dictated. I had become familiar with the property and its history but had an extremely rudimentary knowledge of the movie and its impact on the resort. When I came out and took over the bar in the winter of 2015, all of that changed. Suddenly I was out front and center, and everybody I spoke with had questions I was expected to be able to answer. The first thing I noticed was that the guests would ask three different employees the same movie-related question and get three different answers. Many staffers would point to parts of the dining room wall and claim that it was Baby's corner. I thought to myself that this cannot be right. Thereafter I took it upon myself to be the go-to guy regarding all things *Dirty Dancing*, as well as the history of the hotel and its currently offered amenities. I also learned all I could about off-property attractions that guests might find interesting for day excursions. In hindsight, I might have better served myself by having kept my mouth shut.

It wasn't long before the staff at the front desk began sending inquiring guests to me at the bar. "Go see the bartender," they would say. Little did I know how fast that would accelerate. Eventually, during slower periods at the hotel, I developed what I called the nickel tour. I hardly ever got the nickel, but I did get a lot of satisfaction from the guests' enjoyment. The nickel tour was a quick little tour that entailed leading small groups from the bar, through the market, and into the dining room, where I would point out all the sites where they filmed. I would point out the windows to the outside locations and stop at every place in the building proper. Back then, with of course the Chef's permission, I would take the guests into the kitchen and point out Penny's spot. Then the food and beverage director decided that the kitchen portion of the nickel tour had to stop permanently, regardless of the time and volume of business. It seemed arbitrary and maybe even a little capricious, but then, he was the boss. Thus was born the secret tour.

Mike with guests after an impromptu secret tour of the kitchen after hours

For whatever reason, the ban on taking guests to see Penny's spot in the kitchen stood after the food and beverage director's departure. Chef Porterfield however, like me, was always about the guest's experience and enjoyment. So, with his consent, we worked out a plan to allow guests access to the sacred spot in the kitchen. Although I could slip a random guest or two into the kitchen during regular service hours with the Chef's consent, we determined that the best time to bring guests into the kitchen was after hours. I would tell guests who wanted to see Penny's nook to rendezvous in the tavern around ten o'clock, after the kitchen had closed and the freshly mopped floors had dried. By this time all the higher-ups had long since left the hotel, and I would take the group through the dining room and into the kitchen.

It started with the nickel tour. Two or three guests would be secreted in the kitchen. Every one of them would squat down and look up at the camera, doing their best Penny reenactments. But where it really got crazy was during the official *Dirty Dancing* weekends. All day Saturday guests would approach me in ones and twos, or in groups, and inquire if they could have access to the kitchen, specifically Penny's spot. I would assure them that it wasn't possible at the present time, but if they returned to the tavern later in the evening, I would spirit them in. Since I worked the bar at the big dance until midnight, the kitchen tour would start shortly after that. The crowd would sometimes be upward of sixty people. They would assemble in the tavern, spilling out into the adjacent lobby. We would proceed into the dining room, where I would turn on the lights and assure the guests that this was a privilege that very few people were able to experience. Then we walked through the door and went into the kitchen.

At the edge of the cold line, where the salads and desserts were prepared, I would talk to the folks about the setup to the scene. First I would point to the location of the refrigerator that Neil opened before offering Baby beets or cabbage rolls, brownies or leftover rice pudding. I would list all the foods proffered by Neil to Baby, rattling them off to the guests' amusement because I could of course recite the movie verbatim. Again, one thousand seven times of viewing the movie in two years, six months, and two weeks causes some things to be burned into your memory.

One story I would tell the guests in the kitchen that always brought amusement was one the Chef had recounted to me some years earlier. During the filming in the kitchen, Chef Porterfield was sitting in the kitchen office with the

THE TIME OF MY LIFE

executive chef at the time, Jim Meyers. Chef Meyers's food apparently made such an impression on the movie crew that word spread in the entertainment industry, and the actor Don Johnson hired Chef Meyers to be his personal chef. So off to sunny Miami he went, where Don Johnson was still acting in the 1980s hit TV series *Miami Vice*. That, however interesting, is not the story that really piqued guests' interest.

While they were filming the scene, Neil had the refrigerator door open and was asking Baby what she wanted, rattling off myriad possibilities. In the original scene, he asked her if she wanted ice cream after listing the other offerings. While watching from the office, Chef Porterfield shot out of his chair, yelling, "Cut, cut, cut!" Naturally, the movie people were appalled. *What the heck is this guy doing?* they wondered. Then Chef Porterfield pointed out the simple fact that you cannot store ice cream in a refrigerator. After a brief interlude during which the crew talked over the discrepancy, they agreed.

After a quick rewrite, the narrative changed from ice cream to sweet gherkins. For those who don't know (and there were many guests who didn't), sweet gherkins are a variety of pickle. Other suggestions offered by the kitchen staff and adopted by the movie folks included the incorporation of common items that might be found in a resort like Kellerman's in the 1960s. If you look at some of the innocuous props in the kitchen scene, you'll notice a bottle of A.1. Sauce and a box of matzo ball mix, both of which were added at the hotel staff's prompting.

Having divulged all that information, I would finally reveal Penny's spot. Sometimes it got a little rough, as eager ladies would occasionally jostle each other to be the first to get their picture taken in the nook. But mostly it was just amusing. One by one they would make their way down the cold line, sink to the floor, and try their best weeping Penny impression for the camera. I took many of the pictures using the guests' personal cell phones. But many guests were so happy to be there that they couldn't help but smile broadly despite my admonitions to act like they were crying like Penny did. Some were able to, but most could hardly contain their grins.

Then I would point out the cooking line that Neil and Baby walks down to get to the refrigerator and then back down as Baby shepherds Neil away from Penny. It's the same line Johnny walks down to scoop up Penny and carry her and her shoes away.

A secret-tour guest does her best Penny impression in Penny's spot

One last little-known tidbit, unrelated to the kitchen scene, is the title of the movie. When the movie people first came to the hotel they told us that the movie's title was simply *Dancing*, rather than *Dirty Dancing*. Apparently they had the idea that if we knew the actual title, we'd think it was a skin flick and wouldn't allow them to film the movie on the property. There may be some credence to this story. As mentioned previously, many of the people who were there at the time of filming honestly believe that were Mary Moody Northen still alive when the production company found Mountain Lake, she would never have allowed them to shoot the movie there.

6

The Dirty Dancing Weekend Tour

GRAB YOUR ROADIE AND LET'S GO!

Every tour always began with the guests gathering eagerly in the lobby and tavern after breakfast service. The tour would start at ten in the morning, and people ate quickly so as not to miss it. As not only the tour guide but also the bartender, those Saturday mornings would be particularly busy and hectic for me. Lots of our signature Mary on the Mountain Bloody Mary cocktails and mimosas were made in plastic cups, which I called roadies, so the guests could have a nice libation as they strolled the grounds during the tour. When the hour finally arrived for the tour to commence, I would ask over the low din of chatter, "Who's ready to have the time of their lives?" Believe me, everyone was ready by that point.

Mike the Barman kicks off the tour from the steps in front of the tavern

I would then proceed to what I always considered the front door, which led from the tavern veranda out to the steps overlooking the property. I held the door for everyone, greeting and wishing them a good morning as they passed. Many of the guests I already knew, some better than others, from their visits to the tavern after or even before they had checked in the previous evening. Often even the nondrinkers would have passed through the tavern, having been informed by someone that I did the tour and wanting to confirm the proper start time. After the last guest had passed through the door and they all had assembled on the front driveway, I would take my spot on either the second or third step from the bottom so I could be both seen and heard, and then I would begin the tour.

It always started with me informing the guests that the way *Dirty Dancing*'s producers found Mountain Lake was quite remarkable. The hotel had seldom advertised, but for some reason, in 1986 management decided to place an advertisement in an airline magazine. As luck would have it, one of the production staff saw the ad while on a flight to New York. The production team had been searching for a site throughout the Poconos and Catskills, but just as Mr. Kellerman laments to Tito at the season-ending dance about it "all coming to an end," indeed it had by the 1980s. Declining business shuttered many of the old resorts, including Grossinger's Catskill Resort. *Dirty Dancing* writer Eleanor Bergstein said her script was semiautobiographical, a recounting of her summers vacationing at Grossinger's. Upon seeing the Mountain Lake ad, production staff thought it resembled what they had been looking for further north, so they paid Mountain Lake a visit. Once on site, they knew they had found their Kellerman's.

It's at this point that I also let guests know that Mountain Lake wasn't the movie's only production location. Certain scenes were filmed at Chimney Rock Camp, a defunct boys' summer camp in Lake Lure, North Carolina. The camp was slated for demolition at the time but was spared until after the movie wrapped up production there. Essentially, equal amounts of the movie were filmed in each state, half in North Carolina and half in Virginia.

The Lake Lure camp is now part of an upscale neighborhood. The only vestiges of the movie left in Lake Lure are

Welcome to Kellerman's, a.k.a. Mountain Lake

the steps that led from the little bridge up to the Kellerman's employee housing and a few other locations that factored little into the story. All traces of the employee housing, including Johnny's cabin, are gone. Sadly, the barn where Baby carries the watermelon and has her first dances with Johnny is also gone, having been set ablaze by an arsonist several years ago. The steps, as mentioned, are still there, but are on private property, so they can be viewed only from the lake. The little bridge itself was torn apart by movie fans who feared for its safety and took pieces home with them. (As mentioned previously, Mountain Lake has had its share of similar incidents.) The Lake Lure Inn, which had been considered a possible location to serve as Kellerman's, is still there and open to the public. A visitor to the inn can find the stone steps where Baby asks Lisa to cover for her when she's going to dance at the Sheldrake Hotel with Johnny, and the building that served as the dance studio where Mrs. Schumacher drops the purse full of wallets.

The Lake Lure Inn and Grove Park Inn in nearby Asheville had been considered to portray Kellerman's, but they weren't really what the production team had in mind to represent an upstate New York resort in the early 1960s. The scenes filmed at those hotels, along with the Esmeralda Inn, were minimal. Rumbling Bald Resort is also close to Lake Lure. That was the site of the putting green where Marge is lining it up all wrong and Baby asks her dad for the money Penny needs. Despite claims otherwise, the ballroom scenes for both Kellerman's and the Sheldrake were filmed in the Chimney Rock Camp gymnasium, which also is long gone. If you closely study the stonework in Kellerman's ballroom, you'll notice it looks a little fake, and that's because it is artificial. Also, if you look toward the ceiling during the ballroom scenes, you'll notice white sheets hanging. Those sheets were installed to conceal the rafters, which were visible. A gymnasium would have rafters, but an elegant ballroom most certainly would not. Other than these few scene locations, there's nothing else movie-related to see in Lake Lure. Some claim that the iconic lake lift scene with Johnny and Baby was filmed there, but that is demonstrably untrue—more on that later.

Keep in mind, the production company was late in finding Mountain Lake. As such, it was September and October when they filmed here. At the hotel's high elevation (3,900 feet above sea level), autumn comes early, while spring comes late. Because it was September, the grass had started to brown out, while some of the leaves had begun to change with the season. To create the illusion of summer, the movie crew used green food coloring to paint the grass and, where needed for close-ups, some of the leaves on the trees.

WELCOME TO KELLERMAN'S

For the first movie location, you must drive just a little past the hotel on Route 613. There's ample room to turn around either at the road to the hotel's Blueberry Ridge Cabins or at Newport House at the far end of the lake. Driving much farther is ill advised, especially during the winter months, depending on the type of vehicle you have. Driving back toward the hotel after turning around recreates the first view of Kellerman's. The view is much the same, except the horse fencing is gone, the tennis court is now a beach volleyball pit, and swimming pools have been added, which became necessary when the lake decided to go on vacation. (There must be water of some sort during a summer vacation or else the kids' heads will explode.)

Having arrived at the hotel, Dr. Houseman pilots the family Oldsmobile to the front of the old stone lodge, not quite to the front steps and right behind a red Thunderbird. It's here that Lisa indignantly removes her sunglasses and laments that she didn't bring her coral shoes after observing the porter walking past with a sizable stack of shoeboxes. This is when we first meet Mr. Kellerman and Billy. If you look closely, you'll notice that Billy is interested in Lisa, which she doesn't seem to find unsettling. Down on the lawn, Stan, megaphone in hand, announces the planned activities scheduled to take place, interspersed with corny attempts at humor.

The front lawn looks quite different now than as it appeared in the movie. When the movie was made, there was of course no swimming pool. Engineers determined that for the pool to function and not turn into a depository for runoff, the landscape needed to be abridged. That's why the smooth, gentle slope between Baby's Cabin and the hotel seen in the movie has been changed to a terraced landscape. It was graded as such to channel any excess water from heavy rains into the small frog pond between the pool and the gazebo. It's also worth noting that many of the trees visible not only in the arrival scene but throughout the movie are no longer present, many having been replaced by Norway spruce trees, but again, more on that later.

While threading our way down the stairs toward the pool and big chess set, I always liked to converse with the guests about Patrick Swayze. It was then that I would assure them that everybody I ever met who was here in any capacity during the filming of the movie had nothing but positive memories of Mr. Swayze. I could sense a collective expression of joy as they all realized that he was the good person they had all hoped he would be. I would assure the guests that he was a real blue-collar guy, who insisted that he be called Buddy, his childhood nickname.

A view of the Virginia Cottage (back right), a.k.a. Baby's Cabin, in 2017

Back in 1986 the hotel, because of local blue laws at the time, offered only beer and wine to satiate the guests' thirst. That omission of distilled spirits was remedied in 1988, when a group of US senators was to come down from Washington, DC, for a meeting at Mountain Lake. Finding that there would be no scotch, the senators and their staff duly asked the state for a remedy. Virginia legislators readily obliged, passing a bill, which the governor signed, stating that any hotel in the Commonwealth of Virginia could serve liquor by the drink despite any local ordinance, provided the hotel met a few simple requirements: the hotel had to be at least 3,000 feet above sea level, adjacent to a national forest, and within one-half mile of a naturally occurring lake. It so happens that Mountain Lake is one of only two naturally occurring lakes in Virginia. The other is Lake Drummond, in the Great Dismal Swamp near Virginia Beach, which on its best day might be at sea level. Who said government can't get things done?

But I digress. While he was at Mountain Lake, Mr. Swayze was afforded only the options of beer or wine. He would go to the kitchen, where all the alcohol was kept back then since there was no bar at the time (the tavern wasn't installed until 1988, after Virginia's legislative magic), and procure a six-pack of Pilsner Urquell, a Czech beer. He would then, if the weather was pleasant, sit outside on a bench or at a picnic table enjoying his beverage and ask anybody who chanced by if they would care to join him, offering one of his beers. All in all, everybody agrees that Mr. Swayze was a nice, down-to-earth person.

The stone bench by the old shoreline, visible in
the background during the wig scene

BABY'S CABIN

Having reached the giant outdoor chess set of present day, guests' attention would be directed to the old shoreline, which is where the wig scene was filmed. There's a stone bench that can be seen in the film, which is handy as a reference, as it is clearly visible in the background as Dr. Houseman and Max play cards while Lisa and Baby try on various wigs. This area where filming took place was generally neglected by guests, as there was no marker installed and, of course, the Virginia Cottage, a.k.a. Baby's Cabin, is very close.

The Virginia Cottage is among the most photographed structures on the property. I can assure you that on most weekends, *Dirty Dancing* themed or otherwise, the cottage is occupied, having been reserved usually at least a year in advance. There have been guests who have stayed on several days after the conclusion of a *Dirty Dancing* weekend just to stay in the cabin on a Tuesday or Wednesday when it became vacant, just so they could say that they stayed in Baby's Cabin. It's a very nice cottage, and guests do travel from all over the globe to celebrate the movie that means so much to them.

The Virginia Cottage

Guests touring the porch of the Virginia Cottage
on an official *Dirty Dancing* weekend

The cottage is a little different now than when they filmed the movie. Most obviously, the roof is now green and the steps that extended down the front are gone, replaced by a ramp on the side. Now there are also large rocks just below the cabin, on the front facing the hotel, which were not there during filming. The installment of boulders occurred when the pool was constructed and the lawn was terraced. The boulders are there to help shore up the foundation of the cabin since part of the slope it sits on was excavated to level out the pool deck.

The cottage itself has three bedrooms and two doors, both of which face the lake. The second door is the one Johnny knocks on before having the confrontation with Dr. Houseman and storming off. Multiple other snippets of the movie were also filmed in the cabin or on the porch. Baby is seen leaning against the railing, longing for Johnny, shortly before the final dance, and she flits off the porch to check out the main house (i.e., the stone hotel) early in the movie.

The lakeside porch of the Virginia Cottage; the second door is where Johnny and Dr. Houseman exchange unpleasantries

The other scenes at the cottage were filmed inside the cabin. The scene in which Baby gets her father to help Penny after her untoward procedure was filmed in the bedroom located behind the second door, where Johnny and Dr. Houseman confront each other. Two bedroom scenes with Lisa and Baby—one in which Lisa reveals her intention of sleeping with Robbie, another in which Lisa offers to fix up Baby's hair—were both filmed inside the cabin. The "Rainy-Day Game" scene also was filmed there.

Fans will recall that during "Rainy-Day Game" Lisa laments not being able to find her beige iridescent lipstick shortly before Baby hurries off to play charades in the west lobby. For the curious, all evidence points to Baby as the one who committed the lipstick heist. There's a moment during the movie when the song "Hungry Eyes" is playing and Baby is seen applying lipstick while leaning against the railing of the little bridge. She looks around furtively, then pockets the lipstick. Later, after Dr. Houseman has attended to Penny, he scolds Baby, telling her, "Wipe that stuff off your face before your mother sees it." The implication is that Baby is not supposed to wear makeup. Thus is solved the mystery of the vanishing beige iridescent lipstick.

Interior view of the Virginia Cottage, which has three bedrooms

LET'S HEAD LAKESIDE

Because the lake had receded, our next stop on the tour was out in the dry lakebed itself. The mystery of the missing lake is really no mystery at all, as explained earlier. It's a cyclical occurrence. Instead of taking the path that leads directly out into the lakebed, I would walk with the guests down the path in the lakebed that runs parallel to the old shoreline and give them a brief tutorial on the geological history of

Mountain Lake: In 2005 the lake was almost dry, then it returned to almost full pond in 2006 after an exceptionally snowy winter followed by a very wet spring and summer. By 2007 it began to recede again, and it was dry by season's end in 2008. As of this writing in 2022, it was refilling again, at a rate that implies an imminent return to full pond. That's why I would always jokingly tell the guests when they asked what happened to the lake that it was on vacation.

By this point our procession had passed the iconic gazebo. To the right of the path is a small pile of cinder blocks. Many guests assumed that this is the spot where the lift scene in the lake was filmed. Truth be told, that's just where the blocks are stacked now. Over the years the fans have assumed that those blocks were what Patrick Swayze stood on to do the lift. The blocks presently on the lakebed were nowhere around during the filming. For the sake of the guests, the hotel staff have placed blocks out there for years, only to have them disappear. I've seen the blocks stacked in several different locations over the years. The original blocks held down the wooden platform the film crew built for Patrick Swayze to stand on during filming. Like the original blocks, the platform is also long gone.

The actual spot of the famous lake lift scene is to the left of the pathway, about twenty feet away. If you walk around just a bit, you'll find an old cement pad with an iron ring protruding from it. This is an old remnant of the days when it anchored a wooden platform for swimmers. If you stand on, or very near the pad with the ring and angle your body to face northeast, the promontory you see is the same as the one in the background while they are in the lake.

After thirty years, naturally the tree line has changed. Trees grow and they die. The dead trees above the lake line were eastern hemlocks, some of which were nearly three hundred years old when they died. Sadly, they succumbed to an invasive insect, the hemlock wooly adelgid, which is a species of aphid. The adelgid swept through in the late 1990s and early 2000s, devastating the hemlock population. Happily, the hemlocks are on the rebound, and a stroll along any of the twenty-two miles of trails on the property will reveal countless lush, green, young hemlock trees.

Of course, there are folks down at Lake Lure who continue to claim the lake lift scene was filmed in North Carolina. This is patently false. The movie filmed at Mountain Lake for four weeks before finishing shooting in North Carolina. They filmed here during September and October. The lake, even during the height of summer, is a cold sixty-six degrees on the hottest day, so when they shot here in early fall it was cold, cold, cold. Jennifer Grey is reported to have remarked that she thought her nipples might explode because the water was so cold. There was a diver under the water holding Patrick's legs, and the actors were allowed in the water for only around five minutes before being taken to shore and put inside heated tents, rented from a local company in Blacksburg. The producers worried that Jennifer Grey's engorged nipples might change the movie's ratings, but that didn't happen. The cold lake water also caused the actors' lips to turn bluish, which is why they shot no close-ups of them in the water. The site our friends down in North Carolina would have you believe is the spot of the lift scene doesn't fit, if only because there's a mountain in the background that's not in the movie.

Continuing along and carefully threading over the little creeks from the springs and the spongy areas where other springs seep from the ground, we headed to the white boathouse and dock. Past the boathouse, but before you reach the paved walking path, is an underappreciated movie site. There's no placard or marker, but if you look across the dry lakebed toward the gazebo, you'll recognize this area as what everyone refers to as the Creepy Neil spot once they realize where they are. Most guests never recognized this site existed until they were introduced to it. This is where I always jokingly told guests that the greatest line in American cinematography was delivered. With the gazebo lit up with Japanese lanterns in the background, Neil tells Baby how he likes to watch her hair in the breeze, then doubles down with his pompous soliloquy about how he is the most sought-after man in the county, having taken a girl away from Jamie the lifeguard, hence the Creepy Neil moniker.

Having taken our tour this far, we arrived at the Lower Indian Trail, also not demarcated on the hotel guide. The path is far from smooth, with lots of exposed roots and rocks, so if you decide to hike it, look down as much as up lest you trip. But I digress. It's on this trail where Neil and Baby watch Lisa, missing a shoe, follow Robbie out from the fifth tee with its pretty view. Robbie is of course crass and self-serving as Lisa trails behind like a puppy. It's now that Neil utters his great line: "I'm sorry you had to see that, but sometimes, in this world, you see things you don't want to see." He then does the odd segue as he asks her if she wants something to eat.

Following the paved path to the gazebo, we passed the large flat memorial stone the hotel installed in 2009 after the passing of Patrick Swayze. Time and weather have faded the inscription somewhat, but it remains one of the most photographed sites on the property. The stone itself was exhumed from the lakebed, almost from the very spot of the lake lift scene. It seems a little obvious that the memorial rock was the least we could do for Mr. Swayze, considering all that he gave to this world and the attention he brought to this isolated hotel in the Appalachian Mountains. I promise you, if I had a dollar for every time a guest or visitor would jokingly threaten to steal the rock, I would be doing pretty well. I would always assure them that if they could, without mechanical assistance, pick up the rock by themselves and carry it to the parking lot, it was theirs to keep, no recriminations.

Our next stop was the gazebo, where they shot three scenes. Stories vary, but it's my understanding that the movie people didn't like the gazebo the hotel had at the time and had the present gazebo built. There's quite a bit of credibility to this story as, if you stand at the entrance facing the lake, "1986" and the initials of the timber-framing company that built it are engraved along one of the beams. The beam right above the entrance, closest to the hotel, also has "1986" engraved into it, albeit in Roman numerals. There is a less credible story that the gazebo was constructed by Virginia Tech students, or that it was even built in 1985, which judging by the engravings seems unlikely. However the gazebo came into being, when they did film scenes in the gazebo, they made sure to use putty to conceal the engraved numbers and letters.

The gazebo, where three scenes were filmed

Engraved beam in the gazebo indicating the year of its construction, 1986

The first thing visitors notice is the difference between the present flooring of the gazebo and the flooring when the movie was filmed. In the film the floor appears as concentric rings of two-by-fours, while now it's made of large sheets of plywood. Time is hard on everything and everybody, no less so on wooden surfaces exposed to the elements. The original flooring was removed years ago, as it became less and less structurally sound. Admittedly, the plywood flooring is less visibly appealing, but it is functional. Also, the hotel and its 2,600 acres was and remains a nonprofit enterprise. The little money available to work with can be spread only but so far.

The other obvious difference is the stairs, which in the movie lead down to the lake from the gazebo but are now gone. At one time there were boat docks at the bottom of the gazebo steps, but those days have long since passed, and there was no dock when the movie was filmed. When the lake was at full pond, you could walk right down the stairs and straight into the cold waters of the alpine lake. The stairs were removed, and the gazebo's railing was extended to cover the gap left after the steps succumbed to the pressures of the weather. Since there was no longer any lake to walk down into, rebuilding the steps was put on hold until the water level again reaches the gazebo.

There's a little door on the underside of the gazebo. Because I worked so many hours at the hotel, I was often the last employee guests would see before turning in for the night, and I would be there first thing in the morning while they were eating breakfast. They would jokingly ask me if I ever left the hotel. I would in jest assure them that I had a little studio apartment under the gazebo, accessible through that door, but it wasn't what it used to be since the water had receded.

The first scene featuring the gazebo is the merengue lesson taught by a very energetic Penny, shortly after the

Houseman family arrives at Kellerman's. Most of the people dancing in the gazebo were locals, hired as extras, as were most of the people seen later bunny hopping, playing on the lawn, and dining in the hotel. The gentleman whose foot Baby steps on during that early dance lesson, Bob Lilly, has sadly passed away. He taught at the local high school in Pearisburg. In the background is my friend Alice Williams. She traveled down to Lake Lure to be an extra in the final dance scene. And a few years ago, a lovely lady came into the bar with pictures of herself as a little girl with Kenny Ortega, the principal choreographer. She played the little girl dancing in the gazebo, though she wasn't the little girl in the ballroom scenes.

A photo of Bob Lilly and Jennifer Grey between takes
during the filming of the movie at the hotel in 1986

The second scene is the night dance, for which the gazebo was festooned with Japanese lanterns, where Baby stares at Johnny, wishing she were in Vivian's shoes. Max of course impugns Vivian's character to the Housemans while smiling and speaking nicely to her face. Neil leads Baby off, much to the delight of her parents—after all, he is the catch of the county. Later Baby returns to the gazebo, running across the lawn after discovering Penny crying in the darkened kitchen. She manages to get Billy's attention while he's playing records for guests to dance to. Billy pries Johnny away from the lady he's dancing with—who happens to be the "real" Baby, Eleanor Bergstein, the writer of the screenplay—and together all three hustle off to save Penny.

As mentioned previously, hotel management installed placards all over the property to help guests identify the various movie sites. Unfortunately they missed several, mislabeled others, and misplaced one. The misplaced marker is by the chain-linked white posts lining the driveway. Johnny, Billy, and Baby step over the chains as they proceed to the main building. If you look closely, the posts all face the opposite direction now, but more on that later. The placard denoting the crossing of the chains is sited about two hundred feet away from where that scene was shot, which was closer to the gazebo. What's funny about the placards is that years ago the hotel had wooden markers installed, but they all vanished over time. The new ones are all metal and cemented firmly into the ground, so good luck to those seeking to take one home.

The last gazebo scene is when Baby confronts her father as he contemplates not being able to call Baby "Baby" anymore on account of her having been deflowered by Johnny. She implores him not to shut her out, and they both cry before she leaves him alone again with his thoughts. As mentioned previously, it was getting into autumn when they filmed; fall comes early at 3,900 feet above sea level. This is one of the few scenes they filmed at the hotel in which they didn't need to paint the leaves.

A HISTORIC INTERLUDE

Following the gazebo stop on the tour, I would lead guests back to the hotel via the path that cuts across the east lawn and up the wooden stairs. Having this dead time, so to speak, I would give the guests an abbreviated history of the hotel (most of which I've covered in chapter 1). I would point toward the bocce ball court and horseshoe pits and recount how that was the location of the original hotel, the remaining visible rock wall being the old basement, where ice cut from the lake during the cold winter months was stored to provide refrigeration during the spring and summer months.

I would then talk about the few minor skirmishes fought nearby during the Civil War, but how none of them really affected or caused any damage to the hotel. The Civil War itself came to this part of Virginia when Union general George Cook led a small army down from West Virginia with orders to disrupt traffic on the Virginia and Tennessee railroad line. In a sharp skirmish at the Battle of Cloyd's Mountain, General Cook defeated the local Confederate force. Travelers can find a memorial to the engagement on a wayside on Route 100, just outside the town of Dublin, in neighboring Pulaski County.

The Union army thus proceeded over to the nearby riverfront town of Central Depot (now Radford), where they burned the railway bridge over the New River. They crossed the river at a ford known as Pepper's Ferry, not far from where they burned the bridge, and proceeded to Blacksburg. Today a guest can reach Blacksburg in as little as fifteen minutes by car. In the spring of 1864, there being no surfaced roads, it was a different matter. Cook didn't tarry long in Blacksburg. It was an unimportant place at the time—the university was still many years from opening—and he believed that another Confederate force was arriving soon.

General Cook opted to decamp back to West Virginia using the turnpike that led from Blacksburg, over Salt Pond Mountain, where Mountain Lake and the old hotel stood, to Union, West Virginia. A cold, driving rain hampered Cook's progress up the mountain, men, animals, and wagons all floundering in the mud churned up during the steep ascent. The Union forces reportedly found the hotel deserted when they arrived and passed by, leaving the hotel as they found it. About four miles past the hotel, with the going slow because of the muck and mire, and perhaps thinking that the Confederates might be gaining on them, the Union forces started shedding excess baggage.

The site is called Minie Ball Hill, pronounced by the locals as "minnie" but more accurately "min-ay" after the Frenchman who invented the lead bullets that bore his name. Supplies and crates of bullets were dumped over the side of this rough hill to decrease the load and increase the pace. To this day enthusiasts still occasionally find old bullets or other Civil War relics at or near the site. The Union force continued down the turnpike before being intercepted near Peters Mountain, which is the border between Virginia and West Virginia, by a small Confederate unit with a small cannon. After a short fight the Confederates fled, abandoning their brass cannon to Cook.

For decades there was a legend about the cannon. Seems local lore had it that the cannon had been captured earlier and that General Cook, worried about being overtaken by a larger rebel force, put the army's gold into the cannon barrel and sank it in the lake to deny both to the Confederates. That the cannon was captured miles away and that Union records indicate that Cook's force returned with an extra cannon did little to diminish the legend. When the lake drained in 2008, everybody with a metal detector was up in the lakebed searching for the mythical gold. All they found was the last resting place of Samuel Ira Felder.

Samuel Ira Felder of New York fell overboard while boating with his wife and friend on July 23, 1921. Though they searched the lake at the time, his body was not recovered. It would be eighty-seven years until his remains were discovered by chance after the lake drained. It took almost three years of detective work to identify him. Aside from the coins, ring, and belt buckle poor old Ira had when he presumably drowned in the 1920s, about the only thing of value I heard of being found was a quarter. Beyond the recovery of the remains, treasure seekers over the years have returned from their hunt mostly with handfuls of old-style pull tabs from long-ago discarded beer and soda cans.

MEANWHILE, BACK AT THE LODGE . . .

By now the tour would reach the back loading dock area behind the kitchen at the rear of the hotel. I would hop up on
the stone wall and wait for the stragglers to catch up before
continuing with the narrative. I would point the guests to
the trail to Bald Knob, above the hotel, and recount that this
was the path Baby traverses despite the sign on the metal
box (since removed and replaced with a wooden fence) admonishing guests not to go that way. Here she encounters
Billy and helps by carrying one of his watermelons. The
little light posts lining the trail were placed there by the film
crew and taken with them to Lake Lure to help maintain
the illusion that it was all one place.

Mike talking to guests near the back loading dock during a tour

The fence, which partially obscures propane tanks, was repainted several years ago. Before that you could make out the faint outlines of a previous movie marker that denoted that this was the trail to the fictitious employee housing. This sign, like the others, would disappear from time to time, and we eventually resigned ourselves it being a fool's errand to continue to replace it. We decided to mark this spot by installing an Employee Housing sign only on *Dirty Dancing* Themed Weekends. That worked well enough until the weekend when, as I would tell the guests, two mature ladies showed up to steal it at the same time and ended up rolling around in the dirt, pulling hair, scratching and screaming and kicking. After that it seemed best to just leave the space blank.

If you walk up the Bald Knob trail, just a little past the archway, you'll find yourself at the place where Baby makes Johnny crouch down after she sees her father, Lisa, and Robbie emerge from a side door. Of course, Johnny's feelings are bruised because he must hide, while Robbie, who he knows to be a heel, is embraced by Dr. Houseman. Thus, he storms off to seek solace in Penny's cabin. Just a little farther up the Bald Knob trail is a little bridge. In reality the bridge crosses nothing, but some years ago the guys from the maintenance department built it at the behest of Buzz Scanland, the manager of the hotel. Buzz felt that the movie fans would get a kick out of it, and sure enough they did. Over the years countless guests have proudly shown me pictures they've taken on the bridge, recreating Baby's famous pose. More than one guest actually believed that it was the bridge from the movie, which of course it's not. I never led the tour up the path itself because it would have been much too crowded for so many people, but I always encouraged guests to explore it at their leisure.

The side door to the hotel from which Dr. Houseman, Robbie, and
Lisa emerge, as seen from the spot where Johnny and Baby hide

Next I would point guests in the direction of Mary's Barn, which hosts the dance parties on *Dirty Dancing* weekends, as well as receptions and other functions and events. I would then recount the story of the dance floor (since replaced with another floor). Many visitors have assumed that it was the site of the ballroom scenes from the movie, which were of course shot in North Carolina. The dance floor was installed in 2007 by the crew of an English reality dance show based loosely on the movie. Titled *Dirty Dancing, The Time of Your Life*, the show featured young English kids who would dance their hearts out, and at the end of each episode, whichever couple got the lowest score would be excused from the show and driven in disgrace off the mountain in a Barney Fife–style squad car.

Two seasons were filmed at the hotel, in 2007 and 2008, and Miranda Garrison, who played Vivian in the movie, was a judge for both seasons. In 2008 English actress and model Kelly Brook joined the panel of judges. The interesting correlation relates to Kelly Brook's ex-paramour, the actor Billy Zane. Billy Zane was originally tapped to play the lead role of Johnny Castle in *Dirty Dancing* but for some reason never accepted or landed the role. They then tried to cast actor Val Kilmer in the lead, but he passed on the role because he didn't want to be typecast and didn't feel the movie would do well. Instead he took the lead part in the box office dud *Willow*. The producers eventually settled on Patrick Swayze to play the part of Johnny Castle. This raises two questions: First, would the movie have been as successful if anyone other than Patrick Swayze had played Johnny? (The resounding response was no.) Second, do Val Kilmer and Billy Zane ever wake up and ask themselves, "What the hell was I thinking?"

Moving along to the archway, which provides a covered entrance into the hotel lobby, I would explain how the iconic feature was a last-minute addition to the film. Johnny's 1957 Chevrolet Bel Air Sport Coupe was rented from a local man for use in the movie (it was later purchased by a gentleman in Australia). They shipped the car to Lake Lure for further use in the movie before bringing it back to Virginia, where they shot the scene of the car driving the wrong way under the archway to add more material to the film. This explains why the hole in the side window appears different to the hole Johnny originally puts in the window when he and Baby goes to practice their lifts. As the car passes under the archway, a cottage can be seen in the distance. This cottage, Essex Cottage, is no longer standing; it had to be demolished some years back because of structural problems.

The archway under which Johnny drives the wrong way;
it covers the main entrance to the hotel lobby

Aside from the lift in the lake, two other scenes were shot on the hotel property or nearby. The scene in which Johnny and Baby practice running lifts in the field before determining that the best place to practice lifts is in the water was filmed on the old golf course by the Blueberry Ridge Cabins. The other is the log scene.

On the left of the archway is a side door. This is the door from which Dr. Houseman, Robbie, and Lisa emerge, causing Baby and Johnny to duck and hide so their relationship won't be exposed. There is no placard to denote its inclusion in the film. On the right of the archway is another side door, and it's through this portal that I steered guests into the dining room, holding the door for each member of the tour. I would always ask each individual as they passed if they were enjoying themselves or having the time of their lives, to which each person always replied in the affirmative. After the last member of the tour had passed into the dining room I would make my way into the center of the crowd and climb on a chair so that everyone could see and hear me clearly.

A column in the dining room close to the french doors that lead out onto the porch has a marker affixed to it denoting that this is where the Houseman family ate dinner. Actually, almost all of the dining room scenes were shot in this same location, starting with the dinner scene in which Baby wants to send her leftover pot roast to Southeast Asia before saving the world by majoring in the economics of underdeveloped countries. Later, in this same spot, Baby pours the water down Robbie's codpiece after he informs her that some people count and some don't, before he proffers his copy of Ayn Rand's *The Fountainhead*, which he needs back because he has notes in the margin. The Schumachers are sitting in the background, which provides a good point of reference.

The hotel's dining room, where three scenes were filmed

The last scene filmed in this area is the confession scene. The square table has been moved and replaced with a larger, round table, and it is here that Max tells Neil he's going to have to teach him what it feels like to fire an employee. Baby is compelled to confess that it couldn't have been Johnny who stole Moe's wallet because she was with him all night. Johnny doesn't get fired for stealing the wallet, but he does get terminated for fraternizing with the guests—that is, for sleeping with Baby. This would normally be better than getting discharged for theft, but then, in the movie, Baby is seventeen and therefore underage, while Johnny is in his twenties. I acknowledged to guests that this might seem a little creepy, but then, geographically, Mountain Lake is really close to West Virginia, so it's okay. (Even guests from West Virginia would chuckle at that joke.)

Then I would point out the last dining room location. By the kitchen doors is a stone column, and it's by this pillar that Max is browbeating the waitstaff, admonishing them to keep their fingers out of the water glasses and to pay attention to the guests' daughters, even the dogs. Since Baby is watching all of this through the veranda doors and Max looks at her when he remarks about the dogs, it's safe to assume that he's referring to her. Then she sees Johnny for the first time. Along with the rest of the entertainment staff, he emerges through the kitchen doors and walks around the column. Max proceeds to berate Johnny in a manner that seems to imply that they just arrived at the hotel, which always struck me as odd. For decades Mountain Lake Lodge opened to guests around Memorial Day and closed after Labor Day, which was pretty much what most old-style resorts did, fictional Kellerman's included. This was the hotel's season, so why did the entertainment staff apparently arrive with just three weeks left to go until the end of the season? Maybe watching the movie one thousand seven times over the course of two years, six months, and two weeks caused me to overthink things.

Two scenes were filmed on the veranda, or porch as some call it. When they shot the movie in 1986 there were no screens or french doors on the veranda, aside from those that led into the dining room; it was open air all the way across the front of the hotel. The roof was always there since there are rooms on the second floor. The screens and doors were installed in 1988 when the hotel put in the original bar. Back then the present tavern was the library, while the present market was where the original bar was installed. Later the bar was converted into the club room, an annex of the dining room, while the bar was moved over to the veranda in front of the library and renamed Pee-Toots Lounge (a peetoot is a little indigenous frog found and heard only at Mountain Lake). Pee-Toots used to feature black director's chairs emblazoned with the names of Patrick Swayze, Jennifer Grey, and others that were used as bar stools. Like so much else *Dirty Dancing* related at the hotel, they all found their way into someone's trunk and vanished. The library was converted into Stoney Creek Tavern after 2012, when management concluded that people didn't read many books anymore, but they did drink. Books don't help keep the lights on, but liquor sure does.

Baby's director's chair in now-defunct Pee-Toots Lounge

The first time we see the veranda in the movie, Baby has come up to check out the main building. As she strolls slowly along, a soft instrumental version of "(I've Had) The Time of My Life" plays as she passes hanging flower baskets and rows of rocking chairs. This is when she looks through the french doors and observes Max dressing down the wait-staff and first lays eyes on Johnny. Later, the morning after Dr. Houseman attended to Penny's delicate condition, the rocking chairs are gone, replaced by dining tables. Dr. Houseman is obviously not enjoying his breakfast much when Neil comes by to see who's going to be in the big show. At first Dr. Houseman wants to leave early, but he's talked out of it. He leaves, with Lisa following close behind, asking if she should sing "I Feel Pretty," leaving Baby and Marge to finish breakfast by themselves. The table they eat at is at the third window from the left. The placard on the opposite wall mentions the table but incorrectly labels the family as having lunch. I always wondered what kind of maniac has orange juice and grapefruit for lunch.

Occasionally, while I was finishing up the tour in the dining room, I would get lucky and Chef Porterfield would have the misfortune of coming out of the kitchen into the dining room. Since he was one of the few employees left at the hotel who was present when they filmed the movie and was famous for giving Patrick Swayze a ride on his motorcycle, when possible I would put him on the spot and ask him to recount that story and any other tidbits he might care to share. Since by this point the tour was all but completed and he was busy trying to set up for lunch, which followed the completion of the tour, he was ill amused. Being the good sport that he was, and very guest oriented, he always took the time to engage with guests.

UNVEILING THE RELIC

Finally I would conclude the tour, always saying to the guests, "I hope you all had the time of your lives and that you never felt this way before, and I swear it's the truth, or am I just a fool to believe that I had anything you needed, as you all are like the wind." Applause always followed. Following that I would invite the guests into the tavern to receive copies of the old ledger page with Patrick Swayze's signature, if they hadn't already received one upon checking in at the front desk. I also invited them to peruse what I always referred to as the Relic, a copy of the original film script left at the hotel by the film crew back in 1986.

The script was saved from the trashcan when folks down in the executive offices were clearing out decades-old paperwork and they happened to ask me if I might like it, which I definitely did. I would invite guests to look through the script and take pictures holding it. If you ever get the chance to see it, you would be amazed how greatly it varies from the finished product. Especially the ending. Yes, I do have a copy, but no, it's not included in this manuscript—that would be copyright infringement. But if you go to the lodge and ask nicely, they just might let you see a copy.

7

A Tour Guide:
Maps and Scene Locations

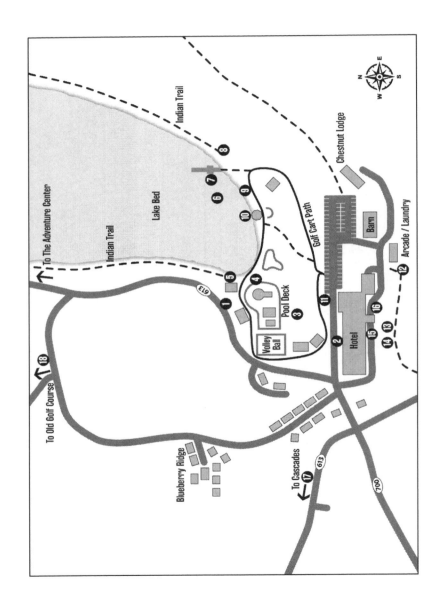

Mountain Lake Property Map Location Key

1 – Spot on Route 613 where the hotel comes into view for the first time as the Housemans approach Kellerman's. The tennis court seen in the movie is now a beach volleyball court.

2 – Where the Housemans park upon arrival and are greeted by Max. The steps in the background lead to the tavern.

3 – The grassy hillside where the guests were playing yard games such as the bunny hop. It is a terraced slope now.

4 – Spot where the wig scene was filmed. The stone bench, visible in the movie in the background, is still there. The new pool deck has partially covered the exact location.

5 –Virginia Cottage, a.k.a. Baby's Cabin. All scenes set in the cabin were filmed here.

6 – Approximate location of the lake lift scene. Sunken cement blocks with iron rings can be found to pinpoint the spot. Also, the hemlock trees on the right shore at the lakebed in the distance match the background in the movie. The cinder blocks lying in the lakebed have no relevance to the film. Despite what the placard may indicate, the blocks are placed there routinely by the staff. I witnessed guests carry off blocks in the past. The fans really will steal anything, nailed down or otherwise.

7 – The boat dock with the boat house is where Neil proclaimed his bona fides to Baby. In the movie the gazebo, lit up with Japanese lanterns, can be seen in the background.

8 – The Indian Trail wraps all the way around the lake and is fairly difficult to traverse because of tree roots and rocks. This is where Baby and Neil see Lisa and Robbie returning from the meeting at the golf course.

9 – Buzz Scanland had the memorial rock removed from the lakebed from the spot of the lake lift and inscribed shortly after Patrick Swayze's untimely death.

10 – The gazebo, built by the production team for the movie, was used for three scenes. The floor is different now, having been replaced several times over the years.

11 – Approximate spot where Baby, Johnny, and Billy step over the chain fence lining the driveway on the way to rescue Penny.

12 – Trailhead for the path to Bald Knob Overlook. During filming there was a metal box with a sign reading "Staff Quarters, No Guests Please." Now there is a fence partially enclosing propane tanks. Baby walks up this trail and encounters Billy. Later Baby and Johnny walk up the path after talking to Neil in the dance studio.

13 – Approximate spot where Baby and Johnny duck down after she sees her father, Lisa, and Robbie exit the hotel.

14 – Location of the bridge over nothing, which was not used in the movie. During his tenure general manager Buzz Scanland had it installed for guests' amusement, and more than a few fans have staged pictures here emulating Baby in the movie.

15 – Side door Baby and Johnny observe her father, sister, and Robbie exit while concealed on the trail above.

16 – Archway covering the main entrance to the hotel, which Johnny drives through with Baby en route to practice lifts. He is actually driving the wrong way, which is not recommended, as there is a blind curve at the end of the hotel.

17 – Route 613, or Doe Creek Road, runs down the mountain to US 460, from which visitors can access the road to Cascades Falls. The log scene was purported to have been filmed on Little Stoney Creek, below the falls. Either way, it's a nice hike and nicer waterfall.

18 – Road to Blueberry Ridge Conference Center and Cabins, which provides access to the road to the old golf course, where the brief field lift scene was filmed. The golf course was not used for the putting green scene in the movie; the course is now a shooting range with a great view.

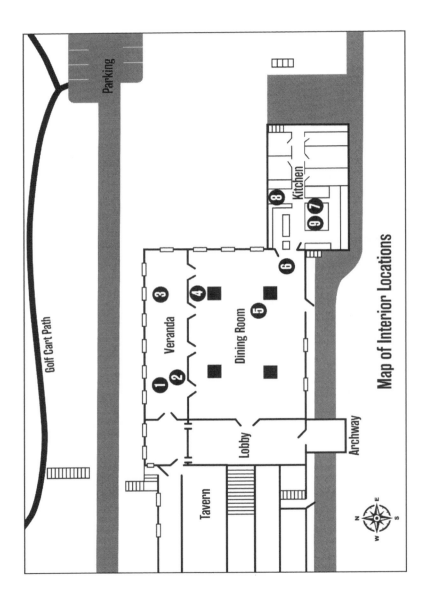

Map of Interior Locations

Dining Room and Kitchen Scenes Location Key

1 – Early in the movie, when Baby leaves the cabin to check out the hotel, she slowly walks along the second-floor veranda, which had rocking chairs staged on it. The current windows and screens were installed after filming.

2 – Baby peers through this set of french doors and observes Mr. Kellerman dressing down the waitstaff. It's also where she first sees Johnny.

3 – For the breakfast scene, set the morning following Dr. Houseman attending to Penny's delicate condition, the rocking chairs have been switched out for tables and chairs. The Housemans dine here, at the second table from the right.

4 – Three dining room scenes were filmed in this spot. In the first scene Robbie is introduced as the Housemans' waiter. In the second, Baby confronts Robbie over the Penny situation, and not appreciating his response, pours water down is codpiece. The Schumachers are visible against the wall in the background. In the final scene the square table has been replaced with a larger, round table. This is when Baby confesses to having spent the night with Johnny.

5 – Spot where Mr. Kellerman is meeting with the waitstaff as Baby watches. Moments later Johnny and the entertainment staff pass by and Max reads Johnny the riot act.

6 – The out door for the kitchen, where Johnny and company enter the dining room.

7 – The end of the kitchen's front cooking line, across from the chef's small office, where Neil offers Baby cabbage rolls, rice pudding, and other cold fare from a refrigerator. Baby looks through the shelves and sees Penny crying. She then leads Neil out of the kitchen. The refrigerator is no longer there. The A.1. steak sauce bottle and other props were suggested by the kitchen staff.

8 –Penny's spot. She's sitting against the wall at the end of the cold line. Later Johnny picks up Penny and her shoes and carries her to the employee barn, presumably.

9 – Baby steers Neil up the kitchen front, or hot line, and away from Penny. Later Johnny and Baby return down this line to rescue Penny.

8

The Rest of the Weekend

Check-in for a *Dirty Dancing* weekend was on Friday, but several guests would arrive on Thursday to familiarize themselves with the property and get a jumpstart on the festivities. The *Dirty Dancing* weekend package included a dinner buffet on Friday night; breakfast, lunch, and dinner buffets on Saturday; and a farewell breakfast buffet on Sunday morning. Between check-in on Friday afternoon and checkout on Sunday morning, the hotel would offer myriad structured activities. The tour was just one of the most popular.

The first diversion was the Friday night dance party, held in Mary's Barn. There was no band, but a talented DJ spun records, both songs featured in the movie and other contemporary and classic tunes. Since many of the guests had traveled great distances, the Friday night shindig wasn't particularly well attended. Many guests had yet to arrive when the dance started at eight, so they would trickle in as the night progressed, many exhausted from a long day of traveling and not up to dancing and twirling around. Not to come off as condescending, but I always likened the Friday dance party to a middle school dance. By that I mean the dance floor was typically not very full and most people just sat and watched from the tables on the periphery. By midnight, when the party broke up, most of the guests had turned in and few were left in the barn.

Over the years the itinerary for Saturday fluctuated. Guests who visited the hotel in the 1990s and early 2000s enjoyed a different experience than those who came in the second decade of the twenty-first century. In 2013 new management inexplicably did everything in their power to sever any connection to *Dirty Dancing*. The gift shop was emptied of anything remotely related to *Dirty Dancing*, the *Dirty Dancing* Themed Weekends were cancelled altogether, and the movie was no longer screened. The new general manager disavowed any connection to the movie and behaved as if they wished it had never happened. That guy didn't last long, and the next general manager quickly moved to reinstate the *Dirty Dancing* connection.

During my tenure at the bar, 2015–2018, the festivities changed almost yearly, sometimes month to month. Aside from the two dances, the only real continuity was the food. The Chef always went above and beyond in his preparation of prodigious amounts of varied and delicious cuisine. Of course, on Saturday night's buffet there was always pot roast—since it was mentioned in the movie it only seemed natural. There was so much wonderful food that the staff and I always eagerly awaited any leftovers there might be.

After breakfast, as mentioned previously, came the tour, for most years. A few years back, however, the innovative staff in the recreation department hit upon the idea of having lawn games. Admittedly the activities didn't quite match those highlighted in the movie. There were no "horseshoes on the south lawn in fifteen minutes," though there are horseshoe pits on the property. The only time I saw any bunny hopping was by guests hamming it up for pictures for the folks back home. Still, it was amusing to look out of the french doors on the veranda and watch the movie fans engage in all sorts of good clean fun. After the introduction of the lawn games, the start of the tour was pushed back to eleven o'clock.

The tour I gave went through many changes. As mentioned earlier, the tour would conclude in the dining room about half an hour before lunch. But following the introduction of the lawn games, the tour would end just as lunch was beginning. It quickly occurred to everyone that it was no longer a good idea to end it in the dining room, as this created hardships for the kitchen staff and servers. Suddenly two hundred–plus people would just sit down or head directly to the buffet. They all needed drinks, and the staff was quickly overwhelmed. After some adjustments, I steered the tour into the dining room from the gazebo, and then, after that presentation, out the side door to the archway, ending the tour at the Bald Knob trailhead, to give the culinary staff a fighting chance to feed the guests. Eventually management decided that the tour was just too big for one person to handle and split it up. I trained a gentleman who worked in the executive office how to do it properly, and come tour time on the *Dirty Dancing* weekends, we would ask the guests to divide themselves into equal groups for the two tours..Oddly, I usually ended up with between seventy and eighty percent of the guests.

After lunch the movie would be screened in the ballroom downstairs. On a few weekends the movie was shown on the giant inflatable screen on the front lawn on Friday night, but the vagaries of the weather and the fact that not all the guests had arrived by screening time put an end to that. Directly after the conclusion of the film, there would be a *Dirty Dancing* trivia contest. I would turn the bar over to a coworker and go downstairs to facilitate the trivia contest, but more on that in chapter 9.

Following trivia, and included in the package, were group dance lessons with the wonderful people from the Sapphire Ballroom, a professional dance studio from the nearby town of Christiansburg. As they arrived at the hotel, I could never help myself and would make comments such as, "Well, if it isn't the entertainment staff," and, "It's the dance people; they're here to keep the guests happy." It was always in good humor. Lane, Debbie, Chris, Dennis, and all the other dancers did a great job and brought a lot of enthusiasm to the weekend.

A lot of guests would forgo the group dance lessons and use the opportunity to explore the hotel property further and more closely, or even venture off the mountain and make their way to the Cascades Falls in search of the location of the log scene. For others, who paid a modest fee, personal dance lessons were available in the barn with the Sapphire Ballroom dancers. For others still there were bingo and board games in the ballroom or the adjacent rooms downstairs. Toward the end of my tenure the hotel introduced a *Dirty Dancing*–themed costume contest. There had always been guests who would attend the dances dressed in '60s era garb, and even a few who would dress as Baby or Johnny, which was entertaining. With the introduction of the costume contest, the number of attendees who dressed like characters from the film quadrupled. Oddly, it was always the folks who dressed like the Schumachers who won.

At eight o'clock it was time for the big dance, and almost every guest was certain to attend. A few guests spent the whole day sitting in the tavern, watching the movie repeatedly (it played about eight times each day) on the TVs, and some would continue to do so while the dance was taking place. I would leave the tavern under the supervision of the second bartender and head out to the barn to run the bar for the dance out of the old beer hut. The beer hut had been built under the covered back porch of the barn many years before to serve beer to guests who attended the Oktoberfest festivities we used to hold. After the dance concluded at midnight, I would return to the tavern and reopen it for the guests who still had some party left in them. I would have preferred to go home, as I had to be back by eight in the morning to serve mimosas and Bloody Marys, but I was in the hospitality business and all about the guests' wants and needs. There were weekends when I would leave at two thirty, only to return at eight.

Debbie, one of the Sapphire Ballroom dancers, teaching group
lessons on a Saturday during an official *Dirty Dancing* weekend

One of the aspects of the big dance that I really appreciated was the Sapphire Ballroom dancers. Having already
taught group and individual lessons, they would stay, eat
dinner with the guests, and then dance with the guests all
night long. Very reminiscent of the movie. I don't know how
they did it. The hotel is old and rustic, not a fancy, modern
resort resplendent with amenities. Rustic also means no air
conditioning. All those swaying and gyrating bodies in the
barn on a warm July night generated a lot of heat. Selling
cold beer and cocktails was so easy it wasn't fair, and I sold
a lot. The *Dirty Dancing*–themed libations were available
along with standard highballs, margaritas, wine, champagne, beer, and ciders. Those with more refined palates,
craving top-shelf liquors or other spirits and cocktails, would
make the short trek back to the hotel tavern to quench their
thirst. They would return to the dance with a roadie—I had
long ago learned that sending guests out of the tavern with

beverages in a glass often resulted in the glass not coming back to the tavern for a long time, if at all.

All night the Sapphire dancers would play out the movie by dancing with any guests needing a partner, and the guests really enjoyed it. One of the reasons the guests were so excited to dance was because of the energy generated by the opening floor show. It really, and I do mean really, got the attendees into a *Dirty Dancing* frenzy. The Sapphire dancers had a whole routine during which all the major songs from the film, albeit shortened for time, were played in order and the dancers would perform a routine choreographed for each song, rotating dancers in and out to keep themselves as fresh as possible. There was a little monologue, a narrative that paralleled the progression of the songs with what would be happening if the movie was playing. The floor show naturally culminated with the song "Time of My Life." It brought everyone to their feet, applauding and cheering, and set the tone for the rest of the evening. Everyone had fun.

Guests enjoying themselves during the big dance on a Saturday night during an official *Dirty Dancing* weekend

I could watch the dance routine because it so captured the guests' rapt attention that the beer hut saw no customers. But after the floor show it got busy, very busy, and stayed that way all night as the dance got lively. There was a DJ again, but few objected to the lack of an orchestra. Those who did take umbrage, which were few and far between, did so from a misunderstanding of the nature of the dance. Here and there, guests would arrive at the dance dressed up, thinking that it would more resemble the dance portrayed in the movie's first ballroom scene, with an orchestra and conductor. That wouldn't have been as much fun. But you can't please everyone all the time, no matter how hard you try. After the dance concluded, again with "Time of My Life," it was back to the tavern for late night and the secret tour.

Back in the early 2000s when I worked in the kitchen (2001–2012), the dance was very different than it was between the years of 2015 and 2018. There was a DJ and a bar, but the bar was set up as a temporary fixture next to the stage where the DJ spun records. There was neither a floor show nor paid professional dancers to act as the entertainment staff, but there was one highlight that delighted the crowd then that the hotel no longer does. At a prearranged time, the DJ would ask the guests to clear the dance floor for a moment. Curious, they would comply, moving off to the wings and leaving the floor empty. Two staff members would pull open the doors to the barn, and Chef Porterfield would roar into the barn on the motorcycle he had given Patrick Swayze a ride on back in 1986. The crowd would go nuts, squealing and cheering. Every lady had to have her picture taken on or next to the motorcycle. Chef Porterfield was always happy to oblige. Several people invariably inquired about buying the motorcycle each *Dirty Dancing* weekend.

Sunday mornings I would be back by eight at the latest, but occasionally as early as seven, because some of the guests required a little hair of the dog after celebrating a little too much at the dance. The guests had seen so much of me over the previous few days that they might have really believed that I had a little room under the gazebo. Many of the departing guests insisted on taking their picture with me, and I of course readily agreed. Hugs were exchanged, and many promised to come back and visit again. Some guests would, before leaving, engage in the final activity offered by the recreation department, a kind of scavenger hunt during which guests tried to locate *Dirty Dancing*–related places based on clues from a prepared list. Then they were gone, checkout being at eleven o'clock. Also gone were most of the *Dirty Dancing*–related knickknacks and clothes sold down in the gift shop. There might have been a stray refrigerator magnet or child-sized T-shirt left on the shelves, but that was about it. I always felt bad for the housekeepers, who had to scramble to clean and turn over the rooms before the guests who would be checking in at four arrived, especially during the summer months, when we were very busy all the time.

9

The Trivia Contest

After lunch on the Saturday of the *Dirty Dancing* Themed Weekends, most of the guests would go downstairs to the ballroom for a viewing of the movie. After the film ended, I'd leave the bar upstairs and head down to run the trivia game. Believe me when I say that many of the fans I encountered knew way too much about the movie, so I had to come up with some pretty tough questions.

To be fair, I would always caution the guests that if they wanted to win the good prizes, they would have to know some obscure details. I'm not a communist, after all—I'm not giving the good swag away for nothing. To keep it even more fair, I also made sure that every guest knew they could win only a certain number of prizes so it would be fun for everybody. There were times when I met guests who knew so much about the minute details of the film that I would jokingly refer to them as members of the high council of the cult of *Dirty Dancing*. More on that later.

So there I'd be, holding a few pages of paper and a microphone, in front of a few hundred people fresh from watching the movie and eager to win some prizes. A few pages were typed, but most were in my generally illegible chicken scratch, which made them difficult even for me to read, especially in the dim light of the ballroom. I would read the questions, and one of the young banquet staff would try as best she could to identify the person with the correct answer. Sometimes that job went to a lovely woman named Peggy, one of the biggest *Dirty Dancing* fans I've ever met. A *Dirty Dancing* weekend frequent flyer, Peggy always tried to rent the Virginia Cottage, and when she did, she allowed other guests to come inside and take pictures. I still owe her a bottle of Moscato wine for all she did for guests out of the goodness of her heart.

The early, easy trivia questions—that is, the ones that had been typed out—had been used for years before my stint as trivia master by the recreation staff who used to run the trivia and tours before my time. They had been taken directly from an old *Dirty Dancing* trivia game the hotel had. I used those simple questions only for the least of the prizes: coupons for ten dollars off a purchase of fifty dollars or more in the gift shop. Like I said, I'm no communist: you gotta earn it. Also, I always tried to caution the guests not to spend too much in the gift shop before the trivia game, because they might just win the very thing they sought to buy or, at the least, might be able to get it at a discount (pretty much everybody received a discount coupon after the game if they hadn't won a prize outright). Thus, on Sunday afternoon, after the guests had checked out and gone on to return to their homes, leaving the hotel fairly empty, the *Dirty Dancing* section of the gift shop had tumbleweeds blowing through it. The shelves and racks would be utterly barren.

Anyway, here are some of the questions I devised to challenge guests. Test your own knowledge, and good luck! (Answers begin on page 103.)

1. What model car is Dr. Houseman driving when he and his family arrive at the hotel?

2. What is the title of the book Baby is reading in the back seat as the Housemans travel to Kellerman's?

3. What is the name given to the character played by the actor Wayne Knight?

4. When the Housemans first arrive, Wayne Knight's character is announcing activities through a megaphone. Where and when does he say the game of horseshoes will be played?

5. What activity does Wayne Knight claim to have for old people?

6. This is one of my favorite questions, and I've phrased it exactly as I would have asked it during the trivia contest:

When the Housemans first arrive at the hotel and Lisa sees the porter carrying the boxes of shoes, which means they are obviously not Lisa's, she exclaims, "I should have brought the corals," to which Marge replies, "But you brought ten pairs." Dr. Houseman then assures her that this not a tragedy, unlike men trapped in a mine or police dogs used in Birmingham, and Baby chimes in about monks burning themselves in protest.

"Butt out, Baby," Lisa replies.

How many boxes of shoes is the porter actually carrying?

This was always a fun question because all the guests would raise their hands in anticipation of a different question, and slowly, as the question unfolded, there would be fewer and fewer hands until there were none.

7. What is Billy's last name?

8. What are the names of the two beers advertised in neon lights in the barn Baby carries the watermelon to?

9. During the wig scene, Robbie claims to drive a specific brand of car, which happens to also be Lisa's favorite. What type of car is it?

10. During the night dance in the gazebo, Max asks Marge if she's going to dance. What type of dance does she say she's waiting for?

11. During the song "Hungry Eyes," Baby is learning the dance routine with Penny and Johnny in the studio. What is the time on the clock on the wall?

12. When Mrs. Schumacher drops her purse full of wallets, Penny and Baby rush to assist her. Who does Mrs. Schumacher claim was a teacher at the dance school she attended?

13. When Baby goes to check on Penny the day after the mambo dance at the Sheldrake Hotel and after

having spent the night with Johnny, he is standoff-ish. What is his excuse for not being able to stay?

14. As it rains outside, Baby and her father are piecing together a puzzle. Lisa, as usual, is looking at herself in a mirror. Lisa begins to wonder aloud about her beige iridescent lipstick and where it might be. What happened to the lipstick?

15. During the same scene, Wayne Knight's character, using the hotel public address system, announces that it's rainy-day game time. What prizes are offered for winning pin the tail on the donkey?

16. One more question regarding the rainy-day cottage scene: When Baby abruptly dons her raincoat to leave, where does she claim to be going?

17. What is the number on the door to Penny's cabin?

18. What is the number on the door to Robbie's cabin?

19. When Baby and Johnny are walking on the path after the confrontation with Neil in the dance studio, who does Johnny claim can get him into a union?

20. What is the name of the union?

21. As Tito and Max talk at the final dance about the past and how it feels like everything is changing, who does Max claim served the first pasteurized milk to the boarders?

22. What is Dr. Houseman's medical specialty?

23. What is the license plate number to Johnny Castle's car?

This last question was always the final trivia question I would ask. I swear you could hear crickets in the ballroom at that point. Correctly answering this last question always garnered the best prize of all offered during the contest. Usually it was a big, fuzzy *Dirty Dancing* blanket. Now, as unlikely as it sounds, the person who inevitably answered the question correctly was the disinterested husband of a fan. I'm not kidding. Eventually a hand would rise, usually far in the back of the room, and a gentleman would rightly guess the license plate number. I suppose the husbands paid more attention to the movie's classic cars than its storyline. Naturally the spouse was very, very happy, emotional even at times. I would like to think that this last question got the husband more than a big, fuzzy blanket.

Trivia Answers

1. Dr. Houseman is driving an Oldsmobile when they arrive at Kellerman's.
2. Baby is reading a book titled *Plight of the Peasant.*
3. Wayne Knight's character's name is Stan.
4. The game is horseshoes, and it will be played on the south lawn in fifteen minutes.
5. According to Stan, sacks will be offered to the old folks.
6. The porter is carrying ten boxes of shoes, the same number that Lisa brought.
7. The last name of Johnny's cousin Billy is Kostecki. It's never mentioned but is listed in the film's credits at the movie's conclusion.
8. The two beers that are advertised are Miller and Pabst.
9. Robbie claims to own an Alfa Romeo sports car.

10. Marge Houseman tells Max she's waiting for a waltz, and for Vivian to maybe pick up her fur stole off the floor.

11. The clock can be seen in its entirety for just a moment, and the time is one thirty-six.

12. Such charm, such charm. Mrs. Schumacher claims that George Burns was a teacher, though she doesn't elaborate as to what he taught.

13. Johnny, clearly uncomfortable, claims that he has dance lessons with the Kramers and that if he's not there they'll kill each other.

14. Simple: Baby took the lipstick. We solved that mystery back in the "Baby's Cabin" section of chapter 6.

15. Stan offers either ten boxes of Kleenex or a billy goat to the winner.

16. Baby says she's going to the west lobby to engage in a game of charades.

17. Penny is staying in cabin number 5.

18. Robbie's little love bungalow is cabin number 15, and Lisa obviously disregards that go-away towel, much to her disgust and Robbie's surprise.

19. Johnny's dad has called him and given him the good news that Uncle Paul can get him into the union.

20. Oddly, Johnny is not thrilled to gain admittance into House Painters and Plasterers Local #179.

Fun fact: In the original script, a copy of which was left at the hotel, the union is in Pennsylvania and Johnny uses an expletive to describe the union.

21. According to Max, it was Bubba and Zeyda who served the first pasteurized milk to the boarders. "Lots of changes, Max. Lots of changes."

22. He was a cardiologist. It's hinted at when the Housemans arrive and Dr. Housman asks Max how his heart is.

23. Johnny's license plate, issued by the state of New York, reads SP2201. It's visible fully only when he drives off after getting fired, and partially visible when he breaks his window.

10

Things You Might Have Missed, a.k.a. The Movie Bloopers

Almost every movie, no matter how large the budget allocated for production, contains editing errors. *Dirty Dancing* was most certainly not a heavily financed film, having been shot for under five million dollars. But despite the low cost, it proved to be an immensely profitable film. Let me walk you through some of the editing omissions, and there are quite a few. Once you see them, you'll never miss them again, and there's a distinct possibility that you'll ask yourself, having watched the movie so many times, how you missed these oversights in the first place.

The first blooper is more the result of the low budget than a lapse in the editing room. Originally the role of

Marge Houseman was slated to be played by an actress named Lynne Lipton. Lynne Lipton, who had blond hair at the time of filming, was on the set at Mountain Lake for only a week before she fell ill and returned to New York to recuperate. Kelly Bishop, who was originally cast to play Vivian, portrayed Marge for the better part of the film at the suggestion of Jerry Orbach. She quickly shuffled over into her new role as Lisa and Baby's mother. If you look closely at certain scenes, such as the night dance in the gazebo, you might notice a certain coyness in her eyes. Perhaps that was because she had prepared to portray a vixen and not a wholesome, motherly type.

Lynne Lipton filmed two scenes before taking ill: the arrival scene and the rainy-day game segment in which Lisa bemoans her lost lipstick. They reshot the rainy-day scene in its entirety because they had to, naturally, but the arrival scene, not so much. When the Housemans arrive at the front of the hotel, before Lisa complains about not packing her coral shoes after seeing the porter carrying the stack of shoeboxes, we catch a glimpse of Lynne Lipton—ironically, as Lisa whines about the coral shoes and Marge assures her that she brought ten pairs. They reshot the better part of that scene, but in the editing process left just a fleeting glimpse of Lynne Lipton in the finished movie. As the Housemans' car first pulls up in front of the hotel, if you look closely, you'll notice blonde Lynne Lipton in the passenger seat, not brunette Kelly Bishop. Moments later, as the camera pans down behind the Housemans' Oldsmobile, now parked behind the red Thunderbird, if you look through the rear window, you'll notice it's still

Lynne Lipton. Seconds later, as Lisa removes her sunglasses to bemoan her shoe-packing skills, it's Kelly Bishop in the passenger seat.

As mentioned, Kelly Bishop was cast originally to play the role of Vivian but slid over to the part of Mrs. Houseman. What was to be done now? Here they have a low budget film, on location in Giles County, Virginia, which is very rural, and the movie folks are short one of their antagonists, with scant chance of quickly procuring a stand-in. Enter Miranda Garrison, whom we now know as the hateful, selfish, and adulterous Vivian. She had originally been hired as the second choreographer behind Kenny Ortega, but she would end up being so much more. She assumed the role that Kelly Bishop vacated and ended up playing the role of Vivian Pressman memorably.

Seldom in my tenure at the hotel did I hear guests or visitors have any good words for her character. Some even resorted to quite derisive terminology. "Rocket Boobs" was the most common moniker assigned to Miranda's character Vivian, no doubt a reference to the period-piece brassiere she wore while playing the part. We all, however, found Miranda Garrison to be a wonderful lady every time she was at the hotel, even years after the film when she returned for a few stints to serve as a judge on the UK's *Dirty Dancing, The Time of Their Lives* reality show.

Moving along, the film is fairly well edited, considering that the budget was tight and that the production crew had to fuse scene footage from both Mountain Lake and Lake Lure. While not an editing error itself, a lot of fans miss one thing in the movie, starting when Johnny is dancing with Vivian in the gazebo during the night dance. Baby and Neil leave, only to end up in the kitchen, where Baby spots Penny crying on the floor and then leads Neil away. Baby runs back to the gazebo, where she gets Billy to grab Johnny. Most fans assume that Johnny is still dancing with Vivian, but that is not the case. Vivian was wearing a slinky black dress, while the woman he is dancing with then is dressed in white. That lady was not Miranda Garrison, but rather Eleanor Bergstein, the aforementioned screenplay writer who loosely based the story on her own experiences vacationing at Grossinger's Catskill Resort. Ironically, Grossinger's closed its doors for good ("Yes, Max, it really all did come to an end") in 1986, the year they filmed the movie and one year before its release.

One of the most cited gaffes in *Dirty Dancing* occurs during the scene when the song "Wipeout" by the Safaris is playing and Baby dances up the famous stone steps (located at Lake Lure, North Carolina) and on the little bridge. It's often pointed out that her outfit during the same scene goes through a subtle color change, which it indeed does. More often overlooked is the fact that blue jean shorts weren't available in 1963; that abomination was wholly a creation of the '80s, along with mullets and various other fashion misnomers.

The fashion color faux pas is followed not by a blooper but by a bit of unintended movie magic. As the song "Hungry Eyes" plays out to its conclusion, Johnny is trying to teach Baby a bit of the sensuous nature of the mambo while caressing her underarm with his fingers. Her laughter at each of his attempts was not scripted—it seems Jennifer Grey was quite ticklish. They tried to do the scene several times and get one shot where she wasn't laughing, but it didn't work out for a quite a while. The disgusted and exasperated look on Patrick Swayze's face is quite real. He's not acting, folks. So they decided to leave it in the movie, which admittedly adds charm.

The next blooper is so obvious that when I'd point it out to the guests, they were all shocked that they had never noticed it before. I'm referring to the window-breaking scene after Baby castigates Johnny about not knowing the lifts and the show being only a couple of days away, to which he replies, "Well, let's get out of here." Now to be certain, in the South it does sometimes rain while the sun is shining, but it wasn't raining in Lake Lure the day they filmed the scene. You'll notice that as they first approach the car after leaving the dance barn, Johnny adjusts the collar of his leather jacket as they walk into the "rain." Seeing that he has locked his keys in the car (in the original script he accuses someone else of locking them in there since everyone knows his locks are broken), Johnny turns and walks out of the "rain" to where the sun casts a complete shadow of him, before he proceeds to kick the light post out of the ground. If you listen, you'll hear the light post make an unnatural popping noise, like a cork from a bottle, when it loosens up from the ground. Very odd. He then wrenches it from the hole and walks out of the sunshine and into the rainstorm.

It took Patrick five attempts before he succeeded in breaking out the car window, and if you look closely, you'll notice the hole in the window looks much different as the car passes the wrong way under the arch than it did immediately after he smashed it in with the post. Initially the hole appears fairly clean, almost circular, while moments later it's more irregularly shaped. This is because that seemingly seamless scene was filmed in two different states. The window was broken out in North Carolina, while the archway is the main entrance to Mountain Lake Hotel in Virginia. Since they filmed at Mountain Lake first, before moving on to Lake Lure, it must be two different windows. Promptly following the archway scene, Johnny's Chevrolet Bel Air turns down a country lane, and if you look closely through the windshield, you'll notice that Baby's hair has twice as much volume to it as when she excitedly just told Johnny how wild he is as he's passing under the arch. So obviously Jennifer Grey is not the passenger on that country road.

The log dancing scene that follows was filmed in Giles County, Virginia, though not on the hotel's property. I was told by those who claim to be in the know that they filmed the scene near the Cascades waterfall, which is a few miles down the mountain from the hotel. I always recommended to my guests that it was well worth their time to visit the falls, if only for the natural beauty. Admittedly, it can be somewhat of a strenuous hike (almost two miles each way), but the falls are a wonderful experience. I had guests who ventured down there and returned later, eager to show me pictures of a log they found that they swore was the one used in the movie. I had to bring them back to earth by assuring them that no log lying on its side for thirty years could endure, much less such a weak wooded tree as the tulip poplar Johnny and Baby cavort on in the movie. I'm sure that my revelation about the physics of wood and time did little to stop many fans from returning home and showing their friends and family pictures of a log and swearing that it was the one from the movie.

The other location for the log scene cited by some who claim intimate knowledge of the movie is a small rural farm also in Giles County, in a small village called Newport. If this is indeed the case, then the log scene was filmed on either Sinking Creek or Spruce Run, which are the only two streams in the vicinity. Personally, I don't know, nor can I speak to the veracity of this claim of a Newport film location. What I do know is that Patrick Swayze had suffered a leg injury several years before filming *Dirty Dancing* and that during the filming of the log scene he fell off the log and reinjured his leg. He persevered through the rest of the film, in pain, and the last scene he shot was the season-ending dance during which he leaps off the stage. The production crew figured there was a good chance that he would reinjure himself, which he did, so that's why it was his last scene. More on the final dance later though.

The lift attempts in the grassy field, before Johnny and Baby moved on to the lake lifts, were shot up on Mountain Lake's old golf course, which had closed only a few years before the shooting of the movie. If you look closely, you can see that some of the leaves on the trees in the background had started to change into autumnal colors.

A few minor foibles occur during and after the big mambo routine at the Sheldrake Hotel. The Sheldrake scenes were shot down at Lake Lure, in the old gymnasium at the Chimney Rock boys' camp, the same location for the

Kellerman's ballroom scenes, with minor alterations and very low lighting. The only noticeable Sheldrake snafu is the Budweiser bottle on the table by the stage, which is a little out of place. It appears to be a 1980s vintage bottle rather than one circa the early 1960s, when it didn't occur to Baby to mind being called Baby. The next editing error involves the drive back to Kellerman's from the Sheldrake. If you look at the shifter on the steering column as Johnny pilots his Chevrolet Bel Air, it appears to be in Park rather than any gear that would allow forward motion.

Also noteworthy, though not a gaffe: Johnny peeks at Baby in his rearview mirror as she changes. Kind of creepy. Next, if you look at the back window as the car moves along, the beads of water on the back window do not appear to move in unison with the rest of the car. Then, the windshield wipers seem to be just a little too modern for a '57 Chevy driven in 1963, though I'll admit, that may be a little too nitpicky. Finally, as Johnny pulls into the employee parking area in front of the employee cabins at Kellerman's, the side window that he broke out, now covered in plastic, once again doesn't match up with the hole visible when the car passes under the archway as Baby and Johnny adventure off to practice the lift.

Now we come to what I always refer to as the big three bloopers. But before I get to them, it is worth pointing out that Jennifer Grey and Patrick Swayze didn't get along very well with each other during the filming of the movie. The scene set in the dance studio, in which they end up rolling around on the floor and playing air guitar and such during the song "Love is Strange," was completely unscripted. It seems that the tension on the set had become somewhat thick between the two movie stars, and to help lighten the mood, the director made the two feuding stars watch footage of them auditioning for their respective roles together. Shortly thereafter the two were playing around between takes, with the music still playing, and as good fortune would have it, the camera kept rolling, thus capturing an immortal moment in cinematic history. Some have also argued that the blue jean capris that Baby is wearing are historically inaccurate, but I really couldn't say one way or the other.

Just a few brief moments later, Neil interrupts the two young lovers, mounting the stairs and almost catching them. Our next editing error follows shortly thereafter. As Neil, using his infinite dance knowledge, no doubt acquired at the Cornell School of Hotel Management, bullies Johnny into closing the final show with Pachanga, you'll notice Johnny is holding a stack of records in his hands. Then, as Neil turns to walk away, Johnny visibly puts the stack of records on the nearby record rack. It also is very audible, emphasizing Johnny's displeasure. But just a moment later, as Neil is talking to Baby about getting her money's worth from Johnny (she has), if you watch Johnny's reflection in the wall-sized mirror, you'll see him rack the stack of records for a second time.

The next error really confuses me. If you recall, early in the movie Baby walks up a path behind the hotel after leaving the dance, where she watched Johnny and Penny put on quite a floor show until Max put an abrupt end to it. In that scene Baby passes a red corrugated metal box that has

THE TIME OF MY LIFE

a sign that advises guests that this area is for staff only. Baby disregards the posting and runs into Billy, which results in her subsequently carrying the infamous watermelon. If you revisit that scene, before she encounters Billy and while she's passing the red box, there's no vegetation around the red box. But now, as Baby and Johnny walk past the red box, substantial shrubbery grows there. Where did it come from? I always referred to this as the traveling tree when I pointed it out to the guests watching the movie in the bar.

Following quickly upon the heels of the traveling tree, and the heartfelt emotional dust up on the trail following Johnny's realization that he just might be a plaything to this young rich girl, is one of the weirdest bloopers in the whole movie, one that I call the magical belt. I cannot for the life of me figure out how so many fans, particularly women, missed this most obvious of glitches. With most of the other errors I would point out, the female fans would always claim they didn't notice because they were too busy staring at Patrick Swayze or parts of him. Admittedly, the magical belt does happen quickly, but it still happens in an area I assume most female fans looked at from time to time. As Baby kisses Johnny's shoulder in reconciliation, Robbie walks past and infuriates Johnny by suggesting that he had picked the wrong sister. You can see the rage boiling in Johnny's eyes before he hurdles the railing and proceeds to administer a beatdown on the smug waiter. If you take your eyes off Johnny's face and look down at his nether regions, you can clearly see that his belt is buckled and secure. Yet a split second later, as he starts to grapple with Robbie, his belt is oddly dangling unsecured. A split second later and the belt is again buckled. Hmmmmm.

Then comes the sight that you cannot ever unsee. Literally, once you see it, it will be all you look at during this scene for the rest of your life, and the scene was already quite painful as it was. I've always referred to the song that Lisa sings (or butchers) during the rehearsal scene as "The Ookalaakakaawaacca Song," but this is obviously not the true title. In reality, the song is titled "Hula Hana" and was cowritten by Jane Brucker, who plays Lisa Houseman, and choreographer Kenny Ortega. They cowrote this instant classic while the movie was still being filmed, though it would take Jane Brucker many years to get writing credits for the song. What's even more ironic is how much this ear-bleeding song is relevant to the movie's next puzzling gaffe. The gaffe is not so much an editing mistake as it is a wardrobe failure. Not a malfunction mind you, but a failure. I don't know if it was meant to be some sort of subliminal message or a genuine stitching error, but again, once you see it, it's burned into your retinas for life. I am of course speaking of the notorious "crotch fish."

The camera pans from Neil and Billy, the guy in the Hawaiian shirt playing piano, and the little girl practicing guitar for the final show to Lisa (look for the little girl at the season-ending spectacular as she shuffles off the stage, dejected after Johnny crashes it and brings the revelry to a premature end). Admittedly, Lisa's singing is grating on the nerves at best and her dancing resembles a minor convulsion rather than choreography, but those are not the elements that make this scene so disturbing. It's her short pants. If you defy your basic instincts and look at Lisa's crotch, you'll notice what appears, unmistakably, to be some variety of tropical fish. Closer viewing reveals that it is clearly not a sunfish or any other known specimen (I hope), but it really looks like it's supposed to be taken as a fish. Could it be the result of terrible stitchwork by a myopic seamstress? Oddly, with the rather uncoordinated nature of her dancing, Lisa makes the fish look like it's swimming. Puzzles me to this day.

The next discrepancy is so minor it doesn't surprise me that it's always missed. When Lisa goes to give of herself to Robbie, there's a white towel hanging from the doorknob. Everybody but Lisa seems to realize the symbolism of the white towel for what it is, which is most definitely not a towel of greeting. The anomaly, however, occurs a short time later, when Vivian leaves Robbie's room, which is number 16. Even before Vivian stuffs her nylon stockings into her purse, the white towel is gone. Where did it go? Surely neither Vivian nor Robbie got up after their romp and removed it. As a married woman, she certainly wouldn't want anybody to catch them, even after the deed was done, if she was still there. So who removed it?

Next, after Patrick Swayze has driven off in a cloud of dust, with no regrets, but while his song, "She's Like the Wind," is still playing on the soundtrack and Baby has ceased her reflective moments leaning against the railing of her cottage's porch, we find Baby dressing for the final show. Lisa breaks character from her usually dismissive nature and exhibits compassion and concern, offering to fix Baby's hair before she concedes that Baby is pretty just as she is. Now the blooper isn't a big error, but as Baby is about to slip on her nylon stockings, you'll notice that Baby has a big foofy slip on already. Yet at the big final show she obviously isn't wearing it, nor the white nylons she was in the act of putting on when last we saw her. Where did they go? Last minute wardrobe change by Baby? Did her family have to wait for her? Or was it an oversight by the film crew maybe? The big dance was filmed at the site in North Carolina, while the bedroom scene in which Baby is dressing for the show was filmed inside the Virginia Cottage, at Mountain Lake. I think it's a safe guess to call it an oversight on the part of the wardrobe department.

Our tour down editing error lane is about to conclude, as we've reached the big dance, the final show, where people bring their own arrangements. But there are a few more bloopers to come, starting with Johnny commandeering the stage. If you pay close attention, as Baby stands alone in the middle of the stage and Johnny walks the microphone stand to the curtained edge, he begins to remove his leather jacket. A second later, as Billy hurries to place the record on the turntable, Johnny is still wearing the jacket and begins to remove it again, this time succeeding.

Next, as Johnny and Baby are dancing in earnest on the stage, which is the focus of everyone's attention, there's a brief moment when his shirt comes untucked, exposing the flesh on the side of his midriff. Then his shirt is again fully tucked back into his pants, though the pair haven't skipped a beat in their dance routine. Perhaps the magical belt helped. This gaffe is quickly followed by the sweaty-head moment. Looking at Patrick Swayze's head as he and Jennifer Grey glide across the stage, you'll notice that his hair is quite dry. Yet after his dramatic leap off the stage, as he turns to look back at Baby and dance solo down the aisle, his hair is quite drenched in perspiration. This anomaly dates to Patrick Swayze's fall from the log in Virginia. As mentioned previously, the leap was the last scene he filmed, though it did take him several tries to land it right, each one more painful than the last. His head is sweaty because he has been doing everything but leaping to get those shots. The stars and crew of *Dirty Dancing* worked long hours to complete the film in a relatively short amount of time.

Last are the dirty knees. Johnny, having danced his way down the aisle, falls to his knees, pivoting and gyrating on the floor for a moment. When he pops back up to his feet, if you look at the knees of his pants, there's a whitish residue on both his knees. Moments later, as he dances back up the aisle toward Baby, followed closely by the staff kids, his pants are back to a pristine state. Then, briefly, his shirt once again becomes untucked in the same place it had earlier, once more exposing skin, before retucking itself just in time for him to catch Baby for the movie's climactic and iconic lift scene. Johnny truly did own one magical belt.

I must admit I learned of several of the bloopers and miscues from zealous fans over the years, and I learned about a couple from the staff at the hotel. Shout out to Mikey J. for catching the dirty knees. The rest I noticed myself. After viewing the movie one thousand seven times over the course of two years, six months, and two weeks, naturally I ceased to watch the movie and paid more attention to the cinematography as opposed to the story line. There are probably more errors, so maybe this chapter has inspired you to see if you can find any that might have been missed. Have fun. You are, after all, never supposed to have felt this way before.

11

The Day of their Lives and Other Events

Though I can't recall any weddings occurring on any
of the *Dirty Dancing* weekends, there were more than
a few *Dirty Dancing*–themed weddings held at other
times at Mountain Lake Lodge. *Dirty Dancing* themed or
not, every wedding seemed to have one movie aspect in
common: the song "Time of My Life" was played at the
conclusion of every reception, and sometimes several times
during the reception as well. There were up to three weddings each weekend sometimes, but usually there were just
one or two, with each one being different and unique. Some
were country themed, with hay bales and barbecue, while
others ranged from elegant to goth to traditional.

One of the perks of being the bartender was the ability
to get to know the prospective newlyweds and their families. I'd first meet them when they'd tour the hotel while

searching for a venue, then I'd see them again when they returned to sign the paperwork and finalize plans, and then again when they came to have a tasting for the reception menu. One couple visited the hotel a dozen times before their wedding day, searching for the perfect spot on the property for their outdoor ceremony. Because each couple visited so often, if the bride and groom drank alcohol, we were pretty good friends by the time the date of the actual wedding rolled around.

One of my favorites was a wedding for some kids who lived in New York City. They were originally both from rural areas within a hundred miles of the hotel and had met and fallen in love in the city. Both wanted a mountain wedding so their families could easily attend, so they selected Mountain Lake for convenience and its natural beauty. They invited not only their families but also many of their friends from New York. Many of those friends had never been west of New Jersey, and it showed. For the duration of their stay, these city folks, or flatlanders as I referred to all guests from the lower elevations, were perpetually spooked by the sounds of nature. Every nocturnal sound generated by the area's wildlife (and there's a lot) evoked worried looks and questions. Even the hoot of an owl was enough to cause jitters.

One of the noises city guests found most disturbing came from a tiny little frog. A particular species of frog found only at Mountain Lake, known locally as a peetoot, was responsible for so much of these guests' discomfort. Though they're small, there are a lot of them during the summer season. Individually they're not much, but collectively they can put up quite a racket during the night. I'll never forget the evening when one of the New York City guests, obviously unaccustomed to rural life, asked if the croaking sounds generated by the masses of peetoots were from a pack of coyotes. Frogs and coyotes sound nothing alike, but she obviously didn't know. I assured her that it was indeed frogs responsible for the noise, not baying coyotes, but she wouldn't believe me. In her mind there was no way any number of frogs could make that kind of sustained noise. Later she remarked to me how lucky I was to live in a place with so many stars—they didn't have as many back in the city. I assured her that we all had the same number of stars, only you could see more of them at the hotel because there was minimal light pollution, unlike in New York. She looked at me like I was an idiot with drool coming out of my mouth.

Another favorite wedding weekend was the one I refer to as the Italian wedding. The families came from two different states, as well as points in between, making it a destination wedding, though a very well attended one. What a bunch they were, fun beyond belief. They didn't quite drink the hotel dry, but they sure did try. As usual for Saturday weddings, the guests arrived at intervals between Thursday and Friday, drinking moderately most of the time. Saturday was hammer down for this group. Having traveled from afar, they were unfamiliar with the signature craft cocktails we served, but boy did they take to them with relish. I'm not sure exactly what time it happened, but with several hours to go before the nuptials and reception, the grandfather of the bride made a momentous statement. He declared, in the tavern, which was full of wedding guests, that all drinks for anyone going to the ceremony were to be charged to his room, 108. Sure, no problem.

After the ceremony, which was beautiful and touching, I worked the bar at the reception. On the contract, the hospitality bar had a cap of six thousand dollars. Beyond that, the guests would have to purchase their own drinks if they wanted to continue consuming alcohol. They were not drinking cheap rail liquor either. Absolut, Jameson, Beam, Jack, and Captain Morgan were among the midshelf spirits offered at the wedding party. And they drank. And drank and drank. But they were fun—not one angry drunk in the bunch. The banquet manager had to restock my bar so many times he worried that we'd run out of spirits before the reception wound down. What I needed was a fifty-gallon drum of Chianti wine and a pallet of midshelf booze. The six-thousand-dollar cap was hit with about an hour and a half to go before the festivities were slated to end. Normally it would have gone to a cash bar, but the father of the groom, when I apprised him of the impending end to the host bar, said to just let it roll, keep the host bar open until the end of the night. By the time the reception wrapped up the tab was just a tad shy of ten thousand dollars—for a four-hour reception.

Sunday morning I arrived early, as usual. Most of the wedding guests had yet to rise, which wasn't unexpected due to the prodigious amounts of spirits they had consumed the night before. Slowly they emerged from their rooms as the morning passed, making their way into the dining room in pairs or small groups, looking for breakfast. They required Bloody Marys and mimosas, along with food. A

THE TIME OF MY LIFE

little hair of the dog, I assumed—a lot of them looked a little rough around the edges, so to speak. But what tickled me the most was running into the bride's grandfather at the front desk, where he was checking out. He was looking at his final bill and shaking his head slowly. I inquired if everything was okay with him. He replied that he wished that he had said to have all the drinks he said to charge to his room, 108, charged to room 106. His bar bill for just those four hours before the wedding ceremony totaled a little shy of three thousand dollars.

One last wedding that really sticks out in my memory was the one I refer to as the California wedding. It was memorable not for the drinking, which they did a good bit of, but for the cultural differences. The bride had booked, sight unseen using the hotel website, her wedding at Mountain Lake. It didn't take long to surmise that none of the guests had ever been to the South and that most had never been east of the Rocky Mountains. They were genuinely puzzled by southern fare. Grilled pimento cheese? Fried green tomatoes? Pulled pork with vinegar-based barbecue sauce? But it was the sweet tea that really seemed to confuse them the most.

The guests must have driven past billboards while en route from the airport to the hotel (I assume no one drove the thousands of miles), because so many came up to me and asked what exactly sweet tea was. Nonchalantly I would reply that it's iced tea that already has sugar in it. It seemed a concept none of them could wrap their heads around. They would ask why anybody would do such a thing, and I would reply that I didn't know, that's how they did it in the

South when I got here (I was born in Alaska and spent my formative years there before my family moved Florida). I did caution them that the further south you go, the sweeter it gets. Naturally all the guests from California wanted to try the sweet tea, and being in the hospitality business, I obliged. Every one of them was appalled by the sweetness. The kids, however, loved it, chugging it down like it was manna from heaven. When asked to demonstrate how to make the sweet tea so they could recreate it back home for their kids, who had just become instant addicts, the measure of sugar that went into the tea stunned them.

It wasn't all weddings at the hotel aside from *Dirty Dancing* weekends. There were multiple group events that really stand out. My all-time favorite was the *Game of Thrones* fans, who for a few years held a self-organized convention at the hotel. Initially we didn't know what to expect when we were first informed of their booking the hotel for their convention. All we were told was that there would be one hundred–plus guests who would be roaming the property dressed as their favorite characters from the television show based on the books (or whatever costume they wanted, shout out to you RJ), none of which I had read or seen. But they quickly proved to be incredibly fun, extremely nice, and despite the barbarian costumes, very well mannered. I didn't know what LARPing (live-action role-playing) was until they came, but I saw plenty.

While they were at the hotel, we ordered special craft beer from a microbrewery in Cooperstown, New York. We replaced our usual Virginia craft beers on tap with *Game of Thrones*–themed drafts. They had colorful names such as Three-Eyed Raven and Take the Black, which at the time didn't register with me as I had never seen the program. I was disappointed when after two years they didn't return for a third year, but attendance-wise they outgrew our guest capacity.

Mike poses with a Throneser portraying the character
Khal Drogo from *Game of Thrones*

What really sticks out in my memory of their first year at the hotel (and there were a lot of eye-popping moments) was their first night. We used to put on a sprawling seafood buffet in the dining room on Friday nights during the winter and early spring months, which the residents of Giles County loved. The seafood buffet also turned out to be very popular with the Thronesers, as I affectionately referred to them. I was passing through the dining room to the kitchen to get some bar fare for guests in the tavern when a sight caught my eye. Standing in line for crab legs was a local man in a red-and-white checkered button-down shirt, a belt with a large Confederate belt buckle, crisply ironed blue jeans, and cowboy boots. Behind him in line, with an equally empty plate, was a Throneser wearing leather armor, a cape, and a sword.

At that sight, I took a moment to scan the dining room, which was packed with diners. I saw a table with people dressed in overalls and white T-shirts, while at the next table was someone dressed like a tree. Interspersed between tables with locals dressed in what I would call street clothes were tables with Thronesers wearing Viking helmets, flowing robes, princess outfits, and all sorts of colorful garb seemingly straight out of a Renaissance fair. I remember thinking to myself that the locals would be talking about this for a long time to come. Little did I know how right I would be.

During dinner service that evening, with several hours still to go before the conclusion of the seafood buffet, a thunderstorm struck the county. The electricity was knocked out at the hotel and in rest of Giles County. Fortunately the hotel's kitchen appliances ran on propane, so the kitchen could keep serving up shrimp and crab legs and the rest of the offerings. Also, the mountaintop hotel had generators, so despite the blackout down below the lights came back on very quickly inside the stone lodge and everything continued as if nothing untoward had happened.

As was my habit every Saturday and Sunday morning, before heading up the mountain to work I would stop in at the Hilltop, a rural gas station nearby that made surprisingly good food. They also made amazing doughnuts fresh every morning, and I would pick up an assortment on both weekend days to bring up for the hotel staff to enjoy. The morning after the power outage I was loading a box with cinnamon twists, crullers, glazed and jelly doughnuts, and other sweet treats when I overheard two elderly ladies behind me talking about the previous night's storm. One woman remarked to the other something about the inclement weather being caused by "them witches up at that hotel." Her friend responded that the group up there were definitely devil worshipers. At that I turned and interjected that the Thronesers were mostly IT types and just fans of a television program. Unimpressed, they both said in unison, "Satanists!" At that I turned, finished filling my doughnut box, paid, and headed on up the mountain, quite amused.

The first year that the Thronesers were there was memorable enough, but the group that came the following weekend served to prove that you never know who might walk through the doors of the hotel and just how disparate those people can be. The LARPing, swords, shields, horned helmets, and medieval costumes were gone, replaced by leather-clad gentlemen gathered for a European motorcycle conclave. The parking lot, which the previous weekend had been full of cars from a multitude of states, was now overrun with BMWs, Ducatis, and other high-end European motorcycle makes and models. The following year the Thronesers once again returned, but the following weekend the motorcycle people were replaced by a completely different and unexpected group even further removed from Thronesers than the motorcycle group had been: a glee club reunion from a large and prestigious eastern university.

Every year the glee club alumni from this university would gather at a different venue. This particular club had originally formed mid-twentieth century, so the alumni ranged in ages from mid-eighties to recently minted graduates, with a few members who were still enrolled at the university. It was what you'd expect from a multigenerational college social club reunion, so aside from the inordinate amount of scotch consumed, it was a relatively uneventful gathering. Except for one thing: Spontaneously they would break out into song. Groups that were previously chatting would suddenly begin singing in harmony. This happened all over the grounds, constantly. Looking out the window I would observe them engaged in a game of bocce ball one moment, then, not a minute later, they would be huddled up singing and humming in unison. This would occur midmeal in the dining room, men pausing from eating to begin singing together. All weekend long, all over the hotel property, a cappella music could be heard floating through the air.

The glee folks were certainly a big change from both the Thronesers and the *Dirty Dancing* fans, and like both the aforementioned groups, they were entertaining in their own special way. It would take too long and occupy too much space to touch upon all the crazy antics by so many different groups and during so many functions at the hotel. But with events including baby showers and anniversaries, family and high school reunions, bridal showers, weddings, and even team-building retreats, things could and did get a little crazy from time to time. Holiday weekends were also quite hectic, as was Oktoberfest, which was its own rollicking good time. Oh, the memories!

When I mention holiday weekends, I of course mean all the big ones. On Mother's Day and Father's Day, which were very busy for the dining room, the Chef and other kitchen staff would feed hundreds of people, both guests staying at the hotel and those who would drive up for the day, in the space of four hours. On the Fourth of July the hotel would be overflowing with people for the free fireworks display and concerts. It truly seemed like half of Giles County would drive up for the festivities. I would be incredibly busy in the bar because we didn't allow outside alcoholic beverages. The local people seemed to have an affinity for Busch Light beer, which we didn't carry, and I spent the better part of the day having to inform the locals we didn't have Busch Light and I didn't know why we didn't, though I really did know why. Decorum precludes me from stating the actual reason.

Thanksgiving was also a huge deal. In the old days Thanksgiving weekend was when the hotel would close for the season. We had the same families come every year that I was there. They became so familiar to us that we actually framed a group picture of them assembled on the front steps and hung it in the lobby. The Thanksgiving feast itself was massive; some years we fed close to six hundred guests, with all the traditional fare and a dessert selection that had heads swimming.

After we began to stay open until New Year's Day, we added a special Christmas buffet. We also had a very special Santa. When we used to close after Thanksgiving, we had our Santa visit that weekend. After that we added a special brunch with Santa, using the same wonderful gentleman, Bob Evans (no relation to the Ohio restaurant chain). Bob did an incredible job playing Santa. He had been doing it for many years, and many parents who would bring their small children to see him fondly recalled sitting on his lap when they were children themselves. Bob had the patience of a monument. All day long he would sit there and entertain the children, often staying well past the contracted time limit to ensure that every child got their turn to tell Santa what they wanted for Christmas. He gave each child a hand-made deer-antler button, which he pulled from a handmade leather pouch. His costume was unlike any department store Santa: he wore long, flowing robes and carried a hand-carved walking staff. Everybody loved Bob's Santa Claus.

Mike and Santa Bob

New Year's Eve was another special occasion. The new year was rung in downstairs in the ballroom during a gala celebration. The guests would dress up in their finery and be treated to a multicourse dinner of steak and lobsters or roasted fowl. After dinner the revelers would proceed to the ballroom for drinks and dancing into the wee hours. Then the hotel would close for two weeks, opening only on the weekends for guests until mid-March, when the hotel would receive guests seven days a week until the following New Year's Day.

12

Classic Mountain Lake Cocktails

You can't really have the time of your life without a delicious adult libation, now, can you? Guests would always come into the tavern and ask for my best cocktail. I would of course ask them what their flavor profile was and then go from there. During a standard *Dirty Dancing* weekend, we would feature five *Dirty Dancing*–themed drinks. Naturally, I would make the guests anything their hearts desired if they didn't care for the special drinks; I was in the hospitality business after all. Here are the recipes for just a few of the delights I concocted to slake the thirst of the guests. I assure you that the fans loved these drinks, and I'm certain that you will as well.

Mike the Barman strikes a pose after concocting
one of Mountain Lake's signature cocktails

First I need to teach you how to make my special simple syrup and sour mixes. Generally, simple syrup is made with half refined white sugar and half water. I discovered that if I substituted locally sourced clover honey for sugar, it delivered a much smoother and more subtle flavor. I also found that using hot water helped dissolve the honey much more efficiently. As for the sour mix, it consists of two parts honey simple syrup, one part fresh-squeezed lime juice, and one part fresh-squeezed lemon juice, well mixed.

DIRTY DANCING–THEMED COCKTAILS

I'll start with the *Dirty Dancing*–themed cocktails, which were served almost exclusively on the movie weekends for the most part. Two of the drinks, those that I served in highest volume, I would prepare in advance and in bulk—and I do mean bulk. For many, these were girls' weekends away from husbands and kids, and they could get quite libatious.

Lisa's Lemonade

This is the easiest of all the drinks to prepare: it's vodka, lemonade, strawberry syrup, and a nice garnish. This is the small batch version.

Ingredients

- 6 ounces of standard yellow lemonade
- 6 teaspoons of wild strawberry syrup
- 1–2 ounces of strawberry flavored vodka
- 1 edible flower and 1 whole strawberry (garnish)

Method

1. In a separate container combine the yellow lemonade with the wild strawberry syrup to create strawberry lemonade.
2. In a Collins glass, pour an ounce of strawberry-flavored vodka over ice. Add another ounce if you like a little extra kick.

THE TIME OF MY LIFE

3. Fill the remaining space in the Collins glass with strawberry lemonade and stir.

4. Garnish with an edible flower (I used an orchid myself) and a whole strawberry mounted on the rim of the glass.

Notes

- Usually I would just pour the syrup into a large container of lemonade until the strawberry flavor came through in a taste to my liking and the color looked about right. Remember, I was making this stuff in bulk. For some guests I would have to add a little more strawberry syrup to make it a little sweeter for the palate, so if you're making this concoction at home, just go with what you like.

- Enjoy by the glass or by the pitcher. It's a fun, easy summer drink.

Tito Suarez's Margarita

This is most certainly a bulk cocktail that's best if prepared at least twenty-four hours before consumption. This gives the flavors time to marry together. I don't recommend leaving it for more than forty-eight hours before straining out the solids, as the fresh strawberries will start to sour the drink and cause it to turn murky rather than the translucent pink it should be.

Ingredients

- 1–1.5 quarts of fresh strawberries, washed
- 32 ounces (1 bottle) of plain, unflavored tequila
- 2 cans of defrosted frozen limeade mixed with water according to product instructions (usually with 2.5 cans of water)
- 4–5 whole basil cuttings, washed, stems and all
- 13 ounces of simple syrup
- 0.5 tablespoons of store-bought agave syrup (to serve)

Method

1. In a sizable, sealable container, hull and half the strawberries.
2. Add the tequila.
3. Add the limeade.
4. Bruise the basil by rolling the sprigs between your hands until the leaves look, well, bruised. The 4–5 sprigs will generally equal 20–30 whole leaves, depending on their size. Add these to the mixture.
5. Add the simple syrup.
6. Refrigerate the concoction overnight.
7. When the mixture is ready, place a colander over a large serving vessel and strain the mix into it.
8. For each individual serving, fill a standard 16-ounce shaker with ice, add agave syrup and 8–9 ounces of the margarita mix, then cap and shake vigorously.
9. Serve in a margarita glass with a sugared rim.

Notes

- Tito Suarez's Margarita is a great poolside libation.
- You can use either cheap tequila or something up-scale, depending on your preference.

Baby's Punch

This is also a drink best made in bulk. During *Dirty Dancing* weekends we would serve so much of this cocktail that if we were to make them to order, my arms would have gone numb. I inherited this recipe from Carol, who helmed the bar at Mountain Lake for about ten years. I was fortunate to have been able to work with her during her last season there before she retired and moved to a warmer climate. Truth be told, I had to call her from time to time to ask her for refreshers on some of her drinks. For Baby's Punch, I always forgot the grenadine.

Ingredients

- 1 gallon of watermelon vodka
- 8 quarts of white grape juice
- 64 ounces (2 bottles) of triple sec
- 3 cups of grenadine

Method

1. Pour the vodka into a large container (I used a BIG one).
2. Add the white grape juice and triple sec.

3. Add grenadine to taste. Usually about 3 cups of grenadine sufficed for the recipe.
4. Mix very well.
5. Serve over ice in a Collins glass.

Note

- I liked to add a splash of champagne to each drink, but that wasn't in Carol's original recipe. Choose your favorite way to enjoy—there were fans of both versions. Another delightful summer libation.

Kellerman's Cocktail

This *Dirty Dancing*–themed cocktail is not an original drink and takes many names, among them the Peachy Keen and Green Tea. At the hotel, when it wasn't a *Dirty Dancing* weekend, it was on our drink menu as the Peachy Keen.

Ingredients

- 1 ounce of Jameson Irish whiskey
- 1 ounce of peach schnapps
- Sour mix
- Authentic ginger ale

Method

1. Fill a pint glass with ice.
2. Add the whiskey.
3. Add the peach schnapps.

4. Fill the remaining space in the pint glass with half sour mix and half ginger ale.
5. Shake well and serve.

Note

- I always used Maine Root Ginger Brew, but in a pinch Reed's ginger ale works just as well.

One of the problems with making drinks in bulk for special occasions is the risk of leftovers. Unlike the ingredients for soup, alcohol doesn't go bad, generally, so Tito Suarez's Margarita I would sell all summer, even making batches when it wasn't a *Dirty Dancing* weekend. It did indeed sell quite well—so well that during July and August I would sometimes make three batches a week. And yes, I did sometimes have to explain to guests that it was not made with Tito's vodka but with tequila. Very few were ever disappointed by what I served them.

Baby's Punch was a different story however, so I hit upon this last movie-themed cocktail that I served for a week following each *Dirty Dancing* weekend.

Watermelon Crush

Ingredients

- 5–6 small cubes of fresh watermelon
- 3–4 leaves of fresh mint
- 2 tablespoons of simple syrup
- Baby's Punch

- Soda water
- Champagne
- Sprig of fresh mint and a watermelon cube (garnish)

Method

1. In a large stemless red-wine glass, muddle the watermelon and fresh mint.
2. Add the simple syrup and fill with ice.
3. Backfill the glass with Baby's Punch, stopping about an inch from the rim.
4. Top the glass with 2 splashes of soda water and a float of champagne.
5. Garnish with a sprig of fresh mint and a watermelon cube.

MOUNTAIN LAKE SIGNATURE COCKTAILS

Though I thoroughly enjoyed making the *Dirty Dancing*–themed cocktails for the official weekend, I really took pride in the craft cocktails I served both seasonally and year-round. These are the cocktails that kept the guests coming back year after year.

My pride and joy, my true signature drink, was and still is the Blueberry Blast, a.k.a. the Blueberry Mojito. Fun fact: I don't personally care for blueberries. I still have no idea what this drink tastes like. Might as well be an egg to me, only less offensive as it didn't fall out of the backside of a chicken. But people seem to really enjoy it.

THE TIME OF MY LIFE

It was one of the first "wow" drinks. You know, when people try something for the first time and exclaim, "Wow!" It's one of those drinks that when you see it, you ask yourself, "What is that and why am I not drinking it?" If they hadn't seen it, I would introduce it to guests through simple conversation. They would ask me what my best drink was, and I would ask them how they felt about blueberries. I would assure them that it was essentially a health drink and that it just might change their life.

The Blueberry Mojito

Ingredients

- 10–12 fresh blueberries
- 7 mint leaves
- 2 tablespoons of fresh-squeezed lime juice
- 0.5 ounces of simple syrup
- 1 ounce of premium blueberry vodka
- Soda water

Method

1. In a rocks glass, muddle the blueberries, mint leaves, lime juice, and simple syrup.
2. Add the vodka.
3. Fill the glass with soda water till three-quarters full and mix without shaking.
4. Add ice and enjoy.

It's very refreshing, I'm told, but then I wouldn't really know.

The Mountain Sunflower (a.k.a. the Big Dale)

The Big Dale appeared on the cocktail menu as the Mountain Sunflower. The difference in the names is the result of a compromise with the general manager, who found the original name distasteful. Since she signed the checks, I called it whatever she wanted.

The original name came about because of how the drink came about. There was a wonderful, lively couple that had vacationed at the hotel for years, and several times each year, no less. Since they had been such frequent guests, I naturally became very familiar with them. One day Dale, the husband, came into the bar and said to me, "Mike, I want you to make me a drink." Ever the consummate professional, I asked him what he'd like. He replied that he wanted me to make him a drink. Again, I asked him what kind of drink he wanted. Needless to say, we ended up in some pseudo–Abbott and Costello routine for a moment before he articulated that he wanted me to concoct a special drink unique to him. I asked him what kind of liquor he preferred and he said rum. Dale is a healthy-sized man, so on the spot I devised an amped-up rum runner. Thus, a new drink was born.

Ingredients

- 0.5 ounces of Malibu pineapple rum
- 0.5 ounces of Malibu mango rum
- 0.5 ounces of Parrot Bay coconut rum
- 0.5 ounces of Captain Morgan's spiced rum
- 0.5 ounces of Meyers dark rum

- Orange juice
- Pineapple juice
- Grenadine

Method

1. Fill an 18-ounce glass (it's Big Dale after all) with ice.
2. Add the rum.
3. Split the remaining space between half orange juice and half pineapple juice, finishing it with a healthy squirt of grenadine.
4. Stir (carefully) and enjoy.

I stopped after the fifth type of rum only because I noticed the glass was fast running out of room for much more of anything. After adding juice and grenadine, I pushed a straw into the cocktail, offered it to Dale, and warned him it was stout and also an interactive drink—he'd have to stir it himself.

Next, we have some drinks favored more by the gentlemen, though I learned long ago not to pretend to stereotype the guests and their beverages of choice. I've seen many women outdrink their male companions—more than you'd think. After all, either you're a bourbon drinker or you're not. I've also met many people over the years who should not be bourbon drinkers, but I digress.

Hickory Old Fashioned

One spring day during my first year working at the bar, the food and beverage manager for the hotel came up to me and set down a bottle. It wasn't a bottle of spirits, however. He had for whatever reason attended some sort of festival where he came across a vendor selling hickory syrup, which was produced in Highland County, Virginia. He had purchased a bottle of said unique syrup and was challenging me to concoct a drink based on this sticky liquid. Thus was born the Hickory Old Fashioned, my take on the classic.

Ingredients

- 2 maraschino cherries
- 1 thick slice of orange
- 0.3 ounces of hickory syrup
- 1 ounce of Woodford Reserve bourbon, or a comparable brand
- Soda water

Method

1. In a rocks glass, muddle the cherries, orange slice, and hickory syrup.
2. Add the bourbon.
3. Fill with ice to rim and add a splash of soda water.

Notes

- If you don't have access to Highland County syrup, look around for a comparable product. Having retired to Florida, I found actual hickory syrup impossible to find outside of an exhaustive internet search.

Through trial and error, I discovered that adding a few drops of easy-to-find liquid smoke to run-of-the-mill, store-bought maple syrup and whisking them together did the trick. Be sparing with the liquid smoke though—a little goes a long way.

- Instead of bourbon, try it with rye to shake things up.

The Mountain Mule

This is another favorite and the last bourbon cocktail recipe provided here, though there are many more unique mixtures available at the hotel. This cocktail also comes courtesy of Carol and was very well received.

Ingredients

- 1 ounce of bourbon
- 1 ounce of Tuaca (an Italian spirit)
- Sour mix
- Maine Root Ginger Brew or a comparable product

Method

1. Fill a 16-ounce pint glass with ice.
2. Add the bourbon.
3. Add the Tuaca.
4. In the remaining space, add half sour mix and half Maine Root Ginger Brew.

Pineapple Ginger Crush

This is another guest favorite, light and refreshing as well as colorful and perhaps vaguely healthy.

Ingredients

- 5–6 medium pineapple chunks, cleaned
- 3 mint leaves
- 0.5 ounces of simple syrup
- 1 ounce of Malibu pineapple rum
- 0.25 ounces of Parrot Bay coconut rum
- Soda water
- Maine Root Ginger Brew or a comparable product

Method

1. In a Collins glass, muddle the pineapple chunks, mint leaves, and simple syrup.
2. Add the rum.
3. Add a splash of soda and fill with ice.
4. Fill the remaining space with Maine Root Ginger Brew.

Strawberry Cobbler

If you enjoy foofy drinks, here's the one for you.

Ingredients

- Graham cracker powder
- 1 ounce of wild strawberry syrup

- 6 fresh strawberries, washed, hulled, and halved
- 0.5 ounces of strawberry vodka
- 0.5 ounces of vanilla vodka
- Soda water
- Champagne
- Edible orchid and whole, washed strawberry (garnish)

Method

1. First rim the glass. We used a large stemless red-wine glass with graham cracker powder.
2. Add the strawberry syrup and fresh strawberry halves, and muddle.
3. Add the vodka.
4. Add a splash of soda water, then fill with ice.
5. Fill the remaining space with champagne.
6. Garnish with the orchid and strawberry.

Grand Berry Smash

This is the Cadillac of Mountain Lake's refreshing summer libations. It's light and airy as well as colorful and visually appealing. Always the crowd pleaser, both with its delicious flavor and stunning presentation.

Ingredients

- 2 fresh strawberries, washed, hulled, and halved
- 5 fresh blueberries, washed
- 3 fresh raspberries, rinsed
- 2 tablespoons of fresh lime juice

- 0.5 ounces of simple syrup
- 1 ounce of Grand Marnier
- Soda water
- Champagne

Method

1. In a Collins glass, muddle the strawberries, blueberries, raspberries, lime juice, and simple syrup.
2. Add the Grand Marnier.
3. Add a splash of soda water, then fill with ice.
4. Finish with a float of champagne.

Berry Breeze

Another Mountain Lake summer classic, the Berry Breeze was always popular for its fruity flavor and light crispness.

Ingredients

- 3 fresh strawberries, washed, hulled, and halved
- 4 fresh raspberries, rinsed
- 2 large fresh basil leaves, rinsed
- 2 tablespoons of fresh lime juice
- 0.5 ounces of simple syrup
- 0.5 ounces of strawberry vodka
- 0.5 ounces of raspberry vodka
- 0.5 ounces of Razzmatazz Liqueur
- Soda water

Method

1. In a highball glass, muddle the strawberries, raspberries, basil leaves, lime juice, and simple syrup.
2. Add the vodka.
3. Add the Razzmatazz.
4. Fill with ice.
5. Finish with a splash of soda water.

S'mores Martini

The next drink was, thankfully, offered only during the slower winter months, and although I devised it, I hated it. Known as the S'mores Martini, I referred to it as the floor drink. The reason for my disparaging moniker was that all the ingredients were kept in an undercounter cooler, which required me to get down on my knees to gather the spirits. Admittedly, I probably could have tried to store the ingredients in a more convenient place, but I would rather try to talk the guests out of the drink for pity's sake. My efforts always failed—and actually seemed to increase guests' desire for the cocktail. Being hardheaded, I ended up making the floor drink a lot.

Ingredients

- Graham cracker powder
- 1 ounce of chocolate syrup and extra for drizzling
- 0.5 ounces of Godiva Dark Chocolate Liqueur
- 0.5 ounces of dark crème de cacao
- 0.5 ounces of light crème de cacao

- 0.5 ounces of whipped cream vodka
- toasted marshmallow (garnish)

Method

1. Rim a large martini glass with powdered graham cracker.
2. Drizzle chocolate syrup around the interior of the glass.
3. Fill a 16-ounce shaker with ice and add 1 ounce of chocolate syrup, the liqueur, the crème de cacao, and the vodka.
4. Shake vigorously and strain into martini glass.
5. Garnish with a toasted marshmallow on a short skewer.

I used a little butane torch to toast the marshmallow. If female patrons hadn't already ordered a S'mores Martini, once they saw the floor show with the flaming marshmallow they were sold, and their next drink was usually the cocktail that was my nemesis.

Mary on the Mountain

Finally we come to the bells-and-whistles drink, the fabled Mary on the Mountain. This was yet another drink I would prepare for a guest and leave other patrons immediately realizing they were having the wrong beverage. Although they sold best in the earlier hours of the day, I found myself making them throughout the afternoon and well into the night. Even those guests who didn't care to enjoy one late in the day often promised to return the following morning to imbibe, and quite often they were true to their promise.

Heck, I had a patron, a gentleman who was visiting a lady friend in Blacksburg, drive up on a Sunday specifically to enjoy a Mary on the Mountain. Having come from Norfolk, Virginia, he explained to me that he had numerous friends back home who had frequented the hotel. They all had assured him that he would be losing out if he was ever near Mountain Lake and didn't take the drive to enjoy this creation, what they all described to him as one of the best Bloody Marys they had ever had. He was not disappointed.

Ingredients

- bacon salt
- 1 ounce of Absolut Peppar
- 5 drops of Bittermens Hellfire Bitters
- 5 drops of Bittermens Celery Bitters
- 3 ounces of Zing Zang Bloody Mary Mix and extra to top

Garnishes

- 3 green olives
- lime wedge
- 1 whole pickled okra
- 1 large whole pickled jalapeño
- 1 whole pickled peperoncino
- 1 pickled cherry pepper

- 1 strip of cooked jalapeño bacon
- 1 pickled quail egg

Method

1. Rim a 16-ounce pint glass with bacon salt.
2. Pour the Absolut Peppar into the rimmed glass.
3. Add the bitters.
4. Add the Bloody Mary mix.
5. Fill with ice.
6. Add more Bloody Mary mix to bring the fluid level to within 1 inch of the rim. It's important to leave this gap because this is where the bells and whistles go.
7. Skewer the olives and lay the skewer across the rim of the glass. This is important because it will help support the other garnishes.
8. Place the lime wedge on the rim.
9. Mount the okra, jalapeño, and pepperoncini in such a way that all the garnishes are wedged vertically between the lime wedge and the skewered olives.
10. Cap the okra with the cherry pepper.
11. Slide the strip of bacon into the glass.
12. Finish the drink with the quail egg.

Notes

- Bacon salt is available at some grocery stores, many liquor stores, and online. Bittermens Hellfire Bitters is available at specialty beer and wine stores and online.

- Pickled quail eggs can be found in most Asian food markets, while all the pickled vegetables can be found in most better grocery stores. The jalapeño bacon is a little harder to come by, but it really makes the drink.
- Instead of Absolut Peppar, use Tanteo jalapeño tequila for a spicy Maria on the Mountain.

Just when the guests thought their minds had been blown with the jalapeño bacon, I would crown the drink with a pickled quail egg. I'm almost certain that the Mary on the Mountain was the most photographed of all the cocktails served at the hotel, and I ended up in more than a few photos. Even if you don't care for all the items, the flavors need to marry together to recreate the drink, so I recommend that you do as the guests at the hotel did: pick out the parts you don't like after letting it all sit for a few minutes.

If you find that you can't make the trek to the hotel for whatever reason, I hope these recipes will bring some of the experience into your home.

Epilogue

t's been several years since I left Mountain Lake, and unlike Max's lamentations about change during the season-ending show in *Dirty Dancing*, change has been good for the hotel. The lake, diminished for so many years, appears to be not only holding water again but also adding volume, indicating that the dry cycle that occurs every few hundred years could be ending at last. The COVID-19 pandemic of 2020–2021 put a damper on the official *Dirty Dancing* weekends, but the hotel offered Kellerman's packages that though not as grand as *Dirty Dancing* weekends, offered many of the same amenities. Two dear friends of mine at the resort took over the duty of giving the *Dirty Dancing* tours. Devoted fans of the movie and all things Mountain Lake, both did a spectacular job, but I'm not sure who has assumed responsibility for conducting the tours now.

In 2019 a production company from down under came to the mountain to shoot a television program for their domestic market. They were slated to return in 2020, but the pandemic forced them to abandon their plans because of the subsequent travel restrictions. Titled *The Real Dirty Dancing*, the Australian reality program saw eight Australian celebrities—four men and four women who didn't know how to dance—try to learn how in just one week. The celebrities ranged from athletes to actors, and the judges of the show were *Dirty Dancing* superfans. They wrapped up production during a *Dirty Dancing* weekend made more special by the presence of Johnny's Chevy, shipped to the States by its Australian owner, complete with the license plate seen in the movie.

Johnny's Chevy returned to Mountain Lake during production of the Australian show *The Real Dirty Dancing*

While the unfortunate COVID pandemic brought to a screeching halt normal life as the world knew it for too long, at Mountain Lake things continued to happen . . . for a while. As mentioned, the official *Dirty Dancing* weekends were placed on hold like so much else, even after the hotel managed to reopen on a limited basis to guests. The more muted Kellerman's weekends replaced the old festivities for a while, but in 2021 everything was back up and running, and the old *Dirty Dancing* weekends resumed.

Physically the property has seen several changes. A new pool and pool deck were constructed in 2020 to complement the old pool, which is still in use. The new pool somewhat resembles a light bulb and lies astride the route the tour takes, covering part of the area where the wig scene was filmed. The stone bench, visible in the background during the wig scene, was vandalized sometime in the spring of 2020 while the hotel was closed because of the pandemic but has since been repaired.

Up on the old golf course, where Baby and Johnny briefly practice lifts in the field, the ruined clubhouse has been repaired and the course has been converted into a trap-and-skeet range. The spectacular views from the clubhouse are still there of course. Closer to the main building, lots of changes are occurring this very year, in 2022. The little building below the stone lodge, which housed the *Dirty Dancing* Museum, is now gone. It had closed in 2019 but reopened until it was demolished recently. Before acting as a museum, the little building had housed the hotel's recreation office. In its place a two-story appendage to the hotel is being added off the dining room. The addition, which will be called Salt Pond Pub and Dining Terrace, will occupy the small lawn and of course will have a large outdoor seating area on the west side of the building. Though this expansion will add spacious extra seating, it will irreversibly change the iconic look of the hotel.

Another construction project involves building a new gift shop and store, to be called the Shops at Mountain Lake Lodge Retail Center. This building will occupy the area where the bocce ball court and horseshoe pits were for many years. As an aside, just above where the new retail center will be was a long building called Lake View, which served as employee housing before it was converted into an expansive gift shop with other specialty stores. Lake View was demolished in 2012 because of structural problems.

Since the lifting of pandemic restrictions, production crews have returned to Mountain Lake. After purchasing the rights to Australia's *The Real Dirty Dancing*, Fox produced and released in February 2022 a four-episode American version that featured eight stars. This should not be confused with *The Real Dirty Dancing UK*, which was also released in February 2022 but was taped entirely in the United Kingdom. Then, of course, there's the highly anticipated sequel to the original movie, set to star Jennifer Grey and carry the *Dirty Dancing* name and perhaps the subtitle *Return to Kellerman's*. The movie will be set in the 1990s and is slated to be filmed at the hotel in the fall of 2022, with a tentative release date in early 2024. I can easily imagine many of the fans I met over the years wishing they could be extras in the new movie.

"Lots of changes, Max. Lots of changes."

That's a wrap. I hope someday each of you will be able to travel to the beautiful little corner of southwestern Virginia that I came to know and love, and visit Mountain Lake and see the place for yourself and enjoy all that it has to offer. It really will change your life, very much for the better. Until then I hope this book will suffice. I hope you had the read of your life, and you never read like this before, and I swear it's the truth.